Donna,

May your life continue to have many Blessings,

Joan Hov

Purposeful Destiny

Joan Hoey

BALBOA
PRESS
A DIVISION OF HAY HOUSE

Copyright © 2014 Joan Hoey.

All rights reserved. No part of this book may be used or reproduced by any means, graphic, electronic, or mechanical, including photocopying, recording, taping or by any information storage retrieval system without the written permission of the publisher except in the case of brief quotations embodied in critical articles and reviews.

Author photo by Amy Mortensen

Balboa Press books may be ordered through booksellers or by contacting:

Balboa Press
A Division of Hay House
1663 Liberty Drive
Bloomington, IN 47403
www.balboapress.com
1 (877) 407-4847

Because of the dynamic nature of the Internet, any web addresses or links contained in this book may have changed since publication and may no longer be valid. The views expressed in this work are solely those of the author and do not necessarily reflect the views of the publisher, and the publisher hereby disclaims any responsibility for them.

The individual experiences recounted in this book are true. The names and descriptive details have been altered to protect the identities of the people involved.

Any people depicted in stock imagery provided by Thinkstock are models, and such images are being used for illustrative purposes only.
Certain stock imagery © Thinkstock.

Printed in the United States of America.

ISBN: 978-1-4525-9286-2 (sc)
ISBN: 978-1-4525-9285-5 (hc)
ISBN: 978-1-4525-9284-8 (e)

Library of Congress Control Number: 2014903263

Balboa Press rev. date: 04/11/2014

For Jesus, my Higher Power, and for Bill and Bill J

Acknowledgments

I thank my husband, Bill, and our son, Bill J, from the bottom of my heart for allowing me to share their personal stories in the hopes of inspiring others. Additionally, I thank the beautiful persons I have been blessed to work with over the span of my clinical career. A very special thanks to Marie Troiano and Brian Wallace, who tirelessly read each of these stories and encouraged me every step of the way.

Contents

Preface xi

Finding Love in Unexpected Places 1
Carl: Learning to Say No 23
Nash Rambler: Follow Your Dream 45
Gabby: Loving Yourself First 67
No Siblings Knocked Down Flat: The Road Doesn't
    End, Take the Turn 91
Wonder Bread: A Father's Second Chance from Heaven 119
The Lake: A Loving Mother Guides and Directs
    from Above 135
The Red Cardinal: A Caring Father Shows His
    Love through Unusual Visits 157

Epilogue 175

Preface

The decision to write this book transpired when my clients, my family, and I began to notice we were being directed toward destinies better for us. It became clear everyone had a purpose, whether it was to be a good parent or a CEO of a large corporation. And they were not mutually exclusive. Often we did not know what our destinies were or when we were supposed to enlarge them, travel to a side road, or even change them altogether. It took courage to leave our comfort zones, even if we were bored to death. Frequently, it was hard to resist reasons to move on. Then, like sailboats moored at the docks, we waited to experience the ocean.

We found that a way to travel in unchartered waters was to widen our minds beyond self—to inch ourselves to a belief in a Higher Power. Some of us already believed in a Higher Power but by different names: Buddha, Mohammed, Jesus, the Greatest Energy, or the Universe. The eight stories of *Purposeful Destiny* relay how the universe prompted and guided us in directions that were for our highest best—through obstacles, unusual circumstances, a strong pull in the pit of the stomach, synchronistic happenings, and the guidance of our departed loved ones.

We discovered no life is without purpose. The mansions of our souls have many rooms. We no longer had to remain in the pantries listening to an endless tape of: "What should I do?" or "No, I can't do that," whatever "that" might be. May we all remain alert to the guidance surrounding us and enjoy the soothing light of destinies fulfilled.

Finding Love in Unexpected Places

In 1986 I was pretty much the sum of what I had accomplished: having taught at the University of Amsterdam, having been on the faculty of Herbert H. Lehman College of the City University of New York, and having created a television program on water purification. But I was not happy. I frustratingly wondered why I did not have a life mate and child. I'd had relationships in the past, but they always ended in disappointment, and I was the one who ended them. Actually, I had already given up on a life mate. When this ache started to consume me, I went to a therapist.

Pete is a big, burly guy with graying blond hair. His office has two beautiful couches and a huge matching chair. I feel nervous. I am trying to calm myself by focusing on the blue-gray pattern of the couches and choosing a small pillow to place behind my back as I sit down on the couch to the right. Pete looks relaxed.

"Joan, tell me why you're here." He hands me a tissue because tears are rolling down my face.

"I guess I thought I would be a mother by now." There is a pause, as I notice a picture of a smiling girl about eight years old. Pete is looking at me with kind eyes.

"Well, why aren't you?"

"I wanted to accomplish certain goals, but I never thought they would exclude my becoming a mother."

"What were the goals?"

I recite my list for him, including two years of traveling in Europe and North Africa.

Pete says in a soft voice: "Joan, you don't have any kids because you haven't wanted any. You practically traveled the four corners of the earth. You put your energies into a lot of other things."

I felt like a rock cracked my skull open. Pete was right. Sobbing, I said, "You're right."

"It's not about me being right; it's about calling it as I see it. We have to stop now, but next time I want to explore why there is not a man in your life."

A week later, as I am sitting in Pete's waiting room thinking about what Pete said, I reflect on my Higher Power. I believe He puts obstacles in my life, but I also believe that He removes those obstacles I have created in order to guide me to a place He knows is best for me. Most of the time I am not aware of the obstacles; sometimes I even like them.

I am waiting for Pete to finish with the client before me. He opens the door with a big smile.

"Hi, big head," he says.

"Hi, smart aleck!" We both chuckle as we sit down. Pete sits down in the huge chair. As he picks up his pad, I notice he is wearing two different socks. I am laughing to myself. Without missing a beat, he gets back to the last question of our prior session.

"So, why isn't there a man in your life?"

"Pete, you're wearing two different socks." I am laughing out loud.

"Yes, I know. It's a game I have with my eight-year-old daughter. She puts two different socks in my shoes on any given day of the week. If I don't see them before I leave the house, she and I go for an ice cream. But let's get back to why there isn't a man in your life."

"Cool about your daughter. I guess I thought to love a man I'd have to find one who was physically attractive first. One that was tall and thin, wore glasses, and looked like a professor. That hasn't exactly worked out, but at least I had the sense to end each relationship."

I am looking at Pete and feeling the texture of the couch with my right hand. He is looking off to the side. He almost looks like he is dreaming when he says: "What was your relationship with your father like?"

"What?"

"Your father. Did you two do things together? Did you talk? Was there anything special that you two shared?"

"No. My father was the 'bank.' He worked a lot."

"I bet he was smart."

"Yes, very, very smart. He only had a sixth-grade education because his father, being a wealthy immigrant and having seen his older sons bomb out of high school, decided that my dad, who was smart enough to skip two grades in elementary school, would go to business school for six weeks."

"How disappointing that must have been for him. What did he end up doing for a living?"

I just love the story I'm about to tell Pete. "Well," I begin, "at first he drove a truck but then decided he wanted to become an insurance agent. So he goes to an insurance company and applies for a job. They say: 'Sorry, you don't have a high school education.' He says: 'I know there's a test; just let me borrow your books and take the test. If I pass, I pass. If I fail, I fail.' He comes home with a stack of books. He asks my mother only to call him for dinner, because otherwise he will be studying in their bedroom. I am amazed that he is studying all day. I only see the door open at dinner. And of course he passes the test and becomes the top agent in his district."

"What do you think the connection is between your father and the professorial type?"

"They both like to study."

"And?"

"They both like learning."

"Yes—but the other important similarity is that they are both distant. Your relationship with your father was remote. After all, he was 'the bank.' Joan, there is a saying: When you did what you did, you get what you got. For a woman with your smarts and experience to exclude the inner qualities from your selection of men means you are getting what you got—no relationship. Think about it."

Feeling angry because he hit the mark, I say, "You're a trip. Next time I see you I'll have a criteria list of all the internal qualities I want in a man." He can see the tears rolling down my cheeks.

"Joan, Joan," Pete says softly, "that would be so, so, so, good."

Walking back to my car parked in front of the drug and alcohol agency where I work as an outpatient therapist, I look at the building and remember that surrender is the theme. Perhaps God wants me to eliminate the physical "requirements" before beginning a relationship. All right, I'll make a criteria list of inner qualities I want in a man. Thinking about the list, my friend Alice comes to mind. She is a fellow therapist. She is tall, thin, and very dynamic. I see her animated face during a conversation we had about decision making. She is saying: "You wouldn't go to a car dealership and buy the first red car just because you liked the color red."

Right you are, Alice! I think to myself. *I have been so stupid.* I realize that I have thought it would be unromantic if I didn't feel an immediate physical attraction to someone. Everything on my accomplishment list is external. They are "head" based. I am a walking "head" with a spiritual life that only registers at 20 percent. What does God want me to learn here? Perhaps He wants me to know a life mate and a child are not intellectual accomplishments. So I begin making a list of the inner qualities

I would find appealing in a life mate. Top on the list is that he must have at least a master's degree, possess a great sense of humor, and be interested in a variety of things. My mind goes on and on compiling the qualities.

I continue to see Pete. He is impressed when I show him my criteria list. He says: "Goals are important, but these criteria are the first steps in broadening your life by not focusing so completely on accomplishments."

I begin to walk the walk. I agree with Pete about the narrowness of my life. But old ways die hard, even after epiphanies. Sometimes I go on "automatic pilot," my obtain-goal mode. What do I want? I want a baby. Maybe I also want a life partner, but I am still skeptical about that one. So I proceed to adopt a baby. Step one: call agencies to set up appointments. I dial an agency's number but hang up before I even hear a voice on the other end. I am ticked off at myself. I tell myself I am a coward. I know the solution but do not have the courage to carry it through.

Epiphanies are doled out to me but not according to my schedule. My Higher Power knows the best choice in each situation. I learn this happens in His time, when He is sure I am ready. Months later, after the failed call to the adoption agency, I realize my Higher Power wants me to fire the negative committee in my head; the one who says "you're a coward" is the first to go. The committee of negative thoughts with tight-laced shoes and collars up to their chins are sent packing. I did not know this then, but now I think of the disapproving thoughts as the wind and brass instruments in a symphony: flutes, clarinets, French horns, the trumpets, bassoons, etc. It takes energy and discipline to blow them into beautiful music. They cop out and say: "Look, let's just play what we know; anything else takes too much breath and too much effort." But the violins, cellos, and other string instruments want me to carry through the "new way." They are the portals that let God's guidance penetrate. When the bows hit the strings, sound happens. There is not a nanosecond of hesitation.

The wood instruments are in full force. I feel terrified like I was encased in an ice sculpture and could not move. Panicking that my obtain-goal mode has been stunted, I take deep breaths. The thought *You always have options* floats across my brain. I also think of Marge Turcott, a clairvoyant whom Alice had suggested years ago (and who, at the time, I thought was outlandish). Her name stands out in bold letters. Yes, Marge Turcott can help me recapture my usual way of proceeding. Desperation resides in every cell, and I call Marge to schedule an appointment.

A week later while driving to Marge's house I recall my first visit with Marge, which was made on a dare with Alice. I enter Marge's waiting room.

It is a large area with big glass windows looking out over beautiful pastureland. I am shocked to see a priest and a nun among the group in the waiting room. Marge opens the door. She's a tall woman who looks like she's somewhere over fifty. The man she's ushering out appears deep in thought, and his white collar suggests that he is the priest.

"Come on in, she says to me. You probably think this is pretty weird."

Surprised that I am next since there are people ahead of me, I answer automatically. "Okay, yes." I laugh nervously. "I do think it's weird."

"Well, most people do their first time."

She drinks a large glass of water, closes her eyes, and says: "You don't like your father. You feel frightened around him. But, child, he is really a lovely man. He is just frightened himself."

Purposeful Destiny

I am bowled over. I immediately think of what Pete said. When I walk out, Alice sees the expression on my face and says, "I told you so."

"Shut up, weirdo." We hug.

I smile at the memory of Marge and especially the masculine timbre of her voice. It has a gusto like "Hit it, boys. Let's go." I hear the gravel under my car, looking forward to my second visit with Marge, as I park. Marge is as happy to see me as I am to see her.

"Well, child, what brings you here?"

"I am completely disgusted with myself. I made the decision to become a single parent through adoption. But when I called the agency, I panicked and hung up before anyone even answered. I am such a coward. I have the solution but don't have the guts to carry it out."

"Well, there's a reason for that, don't you know. And that is you are putting an obstacle between yourself and a man who respects and admires you—someone with whom you share a wonderful friendship."

My mind starts racing. What man and I have a wonderful friendship? No one comes to mind until I begin to think of people at work. I think of Bill Hoey, my joke buddy, the fellow with whom I share funny anecdotes and stories between clients. I raise my head and looked straight into Marge's big blue eyes.

"Obstacles?"

"Yes, degrees and prejudices. Don't you see that just because this man doesn't have your notions of advanced degrees and professorial dress, you're eliminating him from what might be possible? Don't be frightened. He is a lovely man, this Bill."

"Bill Hoey?" I am truly taken aback.

"Yes, child, you are letting a prejudice about high-level diplomas keep you from this beautiful Bill. So go, child. Let go of this limitation. Go and tap the laughter."

Getting into my car, I think Marge and Pete must be conniving with each other! I shift the gears in my little Renault Le Car and let the image of Bill Hoey cross my mind. He does not wear glasses, he is not thin and elegant, and he doesn't have the professorial beard that has been a given for such awhile. In fact, he wears summer suits in winter and bad haircuts in all seasons. If I think a bit more, I conclude his female ideal is no match for me either: his eyes always get brighter around tall blondes with beautiful hair. My hair is black and frizzy, and I am short.

Marge is right about many things—but probably not this. I am not sure I am meant to have a life partner. I realize Marge's "tap the laughter" means that I need to stop being so judgmental and rigid. I remember the first time I saw Bill Hoey. It was during orientation week at the drug and alcohol facility. The person doing the orientation said, "That's Bill Hoey; he's recovering. He leads a patient orientation group."

I thought, *Great. He is leading a group, and he does not even have a master's in social work. Great.*

The next morning, with Marge's words still resonating in my head, Bill comes into my office before my first client.

"Joan, are you okay?"

"Yeah, why?"

"You look so serious."

I realize I am looking at him very intently. "I do?"

"Yeah. How did the call to the adoption agency go?"

"Oh, please don't remind me. I was a chicken. I hung up before anyone answered. And by the way, thanks for the turkey baster on my door yesterday. You know, it's adoption, not artificial insemination."

"I know, but I was down in the cafeteria talking to Bobby, and I saw it and thought of you."

"Gee, thanks."

His face gets red. "Hey, Yale is playing at the rink tonight."

"Hoey, I think you must love hockey."

"I do."

"Well, it's the fourth time you've mentioned it." Feeling safe, I ask if he wants to go.

"Sure."

"Maybe we should get something to eat before we go."

We are sitting in a basement Japanese restaurant. The tables are fairly close to each other. The waiter has taken our orders, and I'm looking the place over when Bill asks: "Are you a virgin?"

I feel like I am free falling. "I—I'm ... over twenty-five years old. I ... hardly think—"

Bill interrupts. "No ... God. No, I mean I didn't see you at the *Rocky Horror Picture Show* we all went to last night. People who haven't seen it are called virgins."

We are laughing so hard, and tears are rolling down my face. When he stops for breath, I point my finger at him and say, "I guess," trying to catch enough breath to finish the sentence, "you're not a virgin." We laugh so hard the couple at the next table begins to laugh too.

The guy says: "We don't know what you're laughing about, but thanks. It's contagious."

Two nights later and a week after meeting with Marge, Bill asks me to the theater. We agree to meet in the facility's reception area after work. I have Marge's comments in mind when Bill steps off the elevator. He is wearing kids' white plastic sunglasses and a brown tweed coat, which he proudly tells me he has gotten at the Salvation Army. My stomach drops, and I think it's embarrassing. Yet there is something truly genuine about him. He is not embarrassed by his outfit or by the Sober One license plate affixed to his car. Once inside the theater I scan the crowd.

There are older people who are well dressed; even the college students seem to have dressed up.

Perfume and cologne are wafting through the air when I see Barbara, a consultant to the agency and a local fashion plate. She walks over with her date, Scott. I pray Bill does not emerge from the men's room until we have finished with our hellos.

Barbara says, "Oh, there's Bill Hoey."

And when Bill comes to stand next to me, Barbara's eyes get big. "Oh," she says again. This time in a voice an octave higher than it was before. "Scott, this is Bill Hoey."

Bill is totally at ease as he shakes hands with Scott, who is wearing a navy sports jacket, gray slacks, and an expensive shirt. When the soft bell rings to announce the play's start, I am relieved. But there is a part of me that is chuckling. Our seats are in the second row from the stage. As the lights dim, Bill reaches over to take my hand. The wood instruments in my mind's symphony are refusing to play. The string section is going wild. I remember Marge's words and hold his hand back.

I am reviewing the night at the theater in my mind when Pete motions me into his office. He is wearing a red flannel shirt. I am about to ask him if he went hunting this morning, but his back is toward me as he closes his file cabinet. He suddenly asks: "Joan, who did you laugh with in your family when you were growing up?"

"Pete, I think you need a break. This sounds like a disconnect from your last session. The woman who walked out did not look happy. And by the way, did you go hunting this morning?"

He chuckles touching his shirt. "No, just had a hurry-up-and-get-out morning. But who did you laugh with in your family when you were growing up?"

Purposeful Destiny

I am irritated, and he notices it.

"You look angry."

"I am. We have already established my relationship with my father was distant."

"So, who did you laugh with in your family when you were a kid?"

"My mother, sister, and brother."

"Who's missing?"

"Oh," I say sarcastically, "it must be my father."

"Can you recall a time when you decided not to reach out to him?"

Whoosh. Immediately, the following scene plays before my mind. I am nine years old, and my dog, Pepper, dies. I am devastated. Within the next week, my grandmother passes away. We are at my grandparents' house after the wake with all the friends and relatives. My father signals me to go outside with him to get extra folding chairs. When we get to the car, he says: "What's the matter with you?"

"I'm sad because Pepper died."

"Well, he was just a dog. Your grandmother was a person. So get with it."

I decided never to tell my father any true feelings again.

Pete looks thoughtful. "Any nine-year-old would have been hurt, Joan. But you don't have to hold on to that decision. It has kept you away from a lot of good men who may be unlike your father. It has been an obstacle to emotional intimacy with men."

As I walk to my car after the appointment, I wonder if Pete is another one of God's messengers. In the lobby of the agency, I see the twelve steps of Alcoholic Anonymous. The third step (Made a decision to turn our will and our lives over to the care of God as we understood Him.) is blazing neon in my mind. Do I really want to turn my will and life over to God? Do I want to give up the me I've protected and projected all these years? I am wallowing in all this when I recall yesterday's conversation with Dan, a client. He is twenty-four and very shy. He explains to me that he can't go to AA meetings because he's not a slave.

"A slave? What do you mean?"

"You know, that crap about turning my will and life over to God as we know him."

"God does not want you to be a slave unless you want to be a slave."

"Well, I sure as hell don't want to be."

"Good. He wouldn't want you to do anything you don't want to do." Dan looks down. He's rubbing his hands together. I notice an anchor tattoo on his right hand an inch below his knuckles. He looks at me and says: "What do you think God wants?"

"Bear with me, Dan. And I'll try to not make this a sermon."

He smiles, showing tobacco-stained teeth. I use an analogy that I think will resonate with Dan. "I think of my Higher Power as a ship builder. He likes to make ships. He needs people to sail the ships. It's up to me whether I choose to be a sailor."

"So, it's okay to think of God as working on a tugboat—like my friend Jake?"

"Absolutely."

"Jake's a tough son of a bitch."

"Does that bother you?"

"No, no—I wish I could be just like him."

"Good."

"Are you sure my Higher Power won't mind me being tough?"

"Some people think of Jesus as their Higher Power, and He was willingly nailed to a cross. He told the high priests of his day that they were filthy on the inside. He told them straight to their faces that they were hypocrites."

"Yeah, but did he say F-bombs?"

"I don't know."

"Jake uses a lot of F-bombs."

"So?"

"Well, if I use Jake as my Higher Power and I curse, it's okay?"

"I don't think it's a problem."

The next time I meet with Dan he tells me he had gone to several meetings.

Dan's courage helped me let go of some of my fear. Still thinking of the twelve steps, I feel God wants me to sail a different boat. I had put myself on a yacht. Maybe I belong on a small sailboat where I can feel the waves and move with the current. After all, isn't that what Pete is saying? Get rid of the fear wall. Allow yourself to feel the full range of emotion with men.

Pete talks to me about laughing. Maybe he was wearing his invisibility cloak at the Japanese restaurant. I believe God is placing Bill Hoey in my life, but I am frightened to death to date him. He's a recovering alcoholic, sober only three years. Taking a leap of faith and flying by the seat of my pants is terrifying.

I call my mother, hoping she will say, "Oh, he doesn't teach at a university. He's recovering, and that could mean relapse, you know." Instead, she says, "Oh, Joanie, he sounds so refreshing. Praise the Lord, maybe you're not meant to be with what you call a professor type."

I cannot believe what she says. I thought telling her he was a recovering alcoholic with three years of sobriety would bring out her protective maternal side. Instead she says, "Well, good for him; he's probably a wise soul." She must be really desperate for me to find someone, I think. But I know I am the desperate one.

With no little trepidation, I decide to date Bill. I begin to admire his genuineness. There is no pretense about him. If he does not know something, he says: "I don't know." Or he says: "I'm in unchartered waters." He talks about his drinking days: "Yeah, I was the lower companion." He laughs. He's taking one of AA's twenty questions that are listed in the front of the schedule books, this one meaning, "Are you surrounding yourself with people drinking out of brown paper bags instead of froufrou drinks at the country club?" His tone and demeanor are not self-pitying but glowing with the truth that he has surrendered, turned his will and life over to a power higher than himself. Slowly, through Bill, I begin to *feel* what surrender means. It means no cover-up. It means not pretending to be perfect when you really know you are not. It is believing that God knows better than you. It is recognizing He is eons smarter, wiser, and more benevolent than you.

It is a Tuesday morning, and Bill and I are having our usual conversation before the arrival of my first client. Thinking about my observation of his genuineness I ask, "Hoey, have you ever told a lie?"

"I don't think I have to repeat what I said in confession last Saturday."

I put my head down, thinking I've really messed up when I hear him laughing.

"Joan, I didn't go to confession last Saturday. But, of course, back in the day when I was known as Wild Will, I told a few lies."

"Wild Will?"

"Yeah. Will lied. He used to say he was a professional hockey player."

"Wow, but do you occasionally lie now?"

"Do I need to call my attorney?"

"Sorry, it's just that you seem so authentic. You know, no cover-up."

"I did enough cover-up back then to last a lifetime. It's a relief to tell the truth."

"I think I need to go to confession."

We both chuckle. After he leaves, I think about the times I have been less than authentic. I realize I always felt a distance between myself and others when white lies tumbled out of my mouth. I promise myself to be 100 percent genuine.

With my growing admiration for Bill and a lightened load of scary feelings, I think about my father. His modus operandi had been that he knew everything. It was true that he accomplished most of the goals he set for himself. But he lived behind a fear wall. No one got close to him emotionally with the exception of his firstborn, Marie. I have been living his superman—his obtain-every-goal mode—and I want to stop.

I love Bill's spontaneity and his great sense of humor. One night on the phone I tell him I'm getting my hair cut.

"Don't get it cut too short; you'll have to wear a bag over your head."

As soon as I hang up the phone, I start cutting the eyes out of a brown paper bag. The next morning as I'm hiding behind a big plant with a paper bag over my head, the receptionist cues me a nanosecond before Bill signs in. I jump out as he looks up. He laughs, I laugh, and I quickly remove the bag before anyone else sees it.

About six weeks later I am at Bill's house. It starts to snow. I suggest going for a hike up Sleeping Giant Mountain. I am only wearing high-top sneakers, but we go anyway. The snow is falling; we stick out our tongues to catch the cold flakes. While we're walking, I say, "Hoey, I'm not yearning for a philosophical discussion!"

"Oh, I grew up with them. My father and brothers had them all the time. After a while, I find them tiresome. Why do you want to have one?"

"No, I mean I'm happy that I'm not yearning for a philosophical discussion. I always thought those were the kinds of conversations I wanted. But right now I don't want one. I'm happy I'm not missing one."

"Well, if you want one or if I want one, it will just happen. Remember, I've got plenty of practice."

"So do I, hotshot."

We're throwing snowballs, and mine hits his neck. I am delighted. Heading back to his house, we realize we are late for a concert and running late to meet some friends who are joining us. There isn't time to go back to my house to change shoes.

"Why don't we just wrap my shoes in tinfoil and bake them at a low temperature."

Bill laughs as he pulls out the tinfoil. We wrap them up and kiss as we slide them in the oven.

A week or so after the concert while cleaning my bedroom, I come across the criteria list I made for Pete. I chuckle when I see "must have a master's degree." I sit down on my bed and realize that although I have two master's degrees, Bill is slowly teaching me what two universities could not: to not be fearful, to live in the present. I remember the AA acronym FEAR: False Evidence Appearing Real. I substitute *expectations* for *evidence*, which resonates with what is becoming a former way of being for me.

Bill's sobriety is giving him authentic power. His sobriety teaches me reverence. God not only protects me but guides me. Alice, Pete, Marge, and Bill have been stepping stones. I am feeling, not just thinking about, my Higher Power. The image of a vending machine comes to mind. The quarters have gone down the slot—God is always present—there is little to worry about. No, I am not being naïve. I realize disasters will happen and disappointments will occur, but through them my Higher Power is guiding me to my next best stop.

———∽∾⌒⚬⌒∾∽———

When I arrive at work the next day, Bill pulls me aside. "I've been told all administration offices are moving to the first floor, and there is no room for me."

"How can that be true?" I ask. "They just promoted you to director of outreach. It's stupid for your office to be on the fourth floor. What will you do?"

"HP (Higher Power) has a plan."

Later that afternoon I notice John, the janitor, is in his supply room frequently. When I walk off the elevator at five o'clock, I see a carpet rolled up outside the maintenance door. Bill looks at me and winks.

"Your office is going to be the cleaning closet?"

"Yup." There is a twinkle in his eyes.

"I can't wait for the reaction tomorrow."

"Mark (the executive director) knows. He told me if I can fit a desk in there, I can have it."

That's the man I want to be my life mate. A sentence telegraphs across my mind: *I love you, special friend.* With it, comes the understanding that love is friendship. It is experience upon experience like a Greek pastry made with phyllo dough—thin layer upon thin layer building a structure until feelings of friendship outgrow the word itself and become love. Bill is very handsome from the inside out. I find him irresistible. I decide to write a letter to God. When I'm back in my office, I write the letter in a small rose-colored book. I ask for guidance and for a sign letting me know if Bill will be my life mate. I wasn't expecting an apparition or the sky to open, just a small, personal sign that I would understand.

———∿∿⚬⚬⚬⚬⚬⚬⚬∿∿———

It is December 3, 1987. In February 1988 I will have been dating Hoey for a year. I decide I will give him a crest ring for Christmas. I know I cannot afford a "real" crest ring, but maybe a jeweler can engrave the words that came to my mind and etch the crest for the Hoey name. When I get home, I call the New Haven Gallic and Hurling Club. I ask the male voice that answers: "I was wondering if you could tell me how to say, 'I love you, special friend' in Gallic—it's a Christmas present for my boyfriend."

The man shouts away from the phone: "Hey, does anyone know how to say, 'I love you, special friend' in Gallic?" A moment later he repeats the words to me. "Ta Gra Agan Duit Acara Dilis."

"Do you have crests for different surnames?"

"No, but if you go to the Country Grill on Whitney Avenue, they should have it."

I get into my car, hoping I can find this place. I have a terrible sense of direction, and these are the days before MapQuest and GPS devices. Thankfully, I find it and walk in to a crowded, noisy bar. When I finally catch the eye of the barmaid, I ask her about the crests and wonder if I could look at the book. She corrects me right away.

"Oh, no, darling, we don't have a book. But we do have a poster with all the names and crests. It's right up there. If you stand on a barstool, you'll be able to see it."

Grabbing a barstool and lining it up with the poster, I notice most of the people in the Country Grill are men, and the skirt I'm wearing could give them an interesting view from my perch on the stool. My face wears a shade of red fit for the season as I search the poster until I find the Hoey name and crest. Mission accomplished. I imagine Bill's face when he opens the ring—and no, I am not expecting a reciprocal ring or a marriage proposal.

Christmas arrives. The jeweler has been able to etch the Gallic sentence and the crest. We are at Bill's house, sitting in the living room that is beautifully decorated with antiques and warm soothing colors, ready to exchange presents.

"You go first," I say.

"No, ladies first."

"Let's open them at the same time."

Wrapping paper begins to fly. Before looking at my present, I steal a peek at Bill's face. He looks astonished.

"How did you do this? It's a real crest ring. What do the words mean?"

"I love you, special friend," I tell him.

He hugs and kisses me and whispers: "You stole my sentence. I love you, my special friend. Now please open your present."

I open the box and see a claddagh ring. It is two hands holding a heart with a crown on top. Bill says that the hands that hold the heart will reign forever. I tell him his ring is not a "real" crest ring but one that a jeweler scratched in patiently.

"Well, the jeweler must have liked you a lot."

"I think he got caught up in the romance of it," I say. Then I tell him the whole story, including the Gallic Club and the Country Grill. As we're laughing about my adventures at the grill, I tell him my mother would have been proud that I was wearing clean underwear that night.

———

On Memorial Day weekend 1988, I am visiting Bill at his house when he invites me to come downstairs because he wants to show me how the water works in his house. My stomach is churning as he shows me how to turn on the water main and then how to shut it off. Then he proceeds to demonstrate the electric box and switches. I bolt upstairs to the bathroom. If this is the preamble to a proposal, it's the weirdest, most maddening one I've ever heard of. Before leaving the bathroom, I decide two things: one, I have to get out of the house, and two, I won't talk about anything but the Red Sox.

When I come out the bathroom door, Bill decides we should go for a ride. I stick to my Red Sox decision, and we struggle through a litany of stale exchanges. Finally Bill says, "I was wondering if you would marry me."

"Yes, yes," I say as we kiss driving on the connector of Interstate 91. "When?"

"How about February?" he suggests. "I was going to ask you at dinner last Thursday, but you were in a bad mood."

"That's funny. I thought I'd go crazy when you kept talking about how to turn the water on and off."

We had a wonderful wedding. We got married at Dwight Chapel at Yale University. The reception was very special, and we used sparkling apple cider for the wedding toast. Two years later, when our toddler son was pulling things out of drawers, I found the letter I had written to God several years before. Bill and I had wanted to be married on Valentine's Day, but the clerk at Dwight Chapel had had to tell us that the fourteenth wouldn't work, and the next available date was February 18. I smiled when I saw the date in the upper right-hand corner. It was February 18. My Higher Power had given me the sign that Bill was going to be my true life partner.

Carl:
Learning to Say No

Purposeful Destiny

The buzzer in my basement office signals my new client's arrival. I climb the stairs to the waiting room so nicely decorated by Hannah, who owns the building. A young man is standing there, probably in his late twenties, small in stature, with dark hair, clear blue eyes, and a wonderful smile. "Carl?" I ask.

"Yes."

"I'm Joan." I motion toward the door. "Right this way." We walk down the stairs to a large office that resembles a comfortable living room, with a brown corduroy couch and two print chairs. One of the chairs is for me. Carl opts to sit on the edge of the couch. A coffee table keeps the space between us.

"Tell me why you're here; take your time, start anywhere. I will be able to follow what you are saying."

Carl looks earnest and nervous. He presses his fingertips into the palm of his hand. "I just got divorced—well, not just. It was six months ago. My wife's, I mean, my ex-wife's name is Valerie." He shoots me a look after the word *divorce*. "I'm getting the marriage annulled."

I am not surprised. He reminds me of an altar boy who would tend to every detail. In a later session he tells me that every one of his brothers and his grandfather were all altar servers. I nod and say, "Tell me about the marriage."

"Well, I don't know. We just stopped liking the same things. We just drifted ... drifted apart."

"Living like roommates?"

Carl's eyes register acknowledgment. The quarters have gone all the way down the slot.

"She'd do things with her friends, and that was okay with me. I'd do things with my friends. We just drifted," he explains. "She's a wonderful person, but we didn't like the same things. Sometimes ... sometimes—"

"Sometimes what?"

"Sometimes I think I'll always be alone." Carl looks down at his highly polished shoes. He turns toward the lamp, as if it too needed this information and repeats: "Yeah, I think I'll probably always be alone. I keep thinking about the future, and frankly, it's scary."

I make a little line drawing and hand it to Carl:

———————— • ————————

Leaning closer, I say, "The line to the left represents the past. You can glance back, but don't take a long stare back. When we stare backward, we can get overwhelmed. The line on the right side of the dot is the future. Again, you can look ahead, but don't look too hard because it can cause anxiety. The dot is the present. Stay on the dot. When you feel yourself thinking about Valerie, pull yourself back to the dot. Likewise, if you keep imagining the future, pull yourself back to the dot."

"Suppose I can't? You know, my mind just won't stop worrying about how things will be for the rest of my life."

I suggest that he imagine himself pushing the eject button on his remote control and just eject those thoughts. He could also picture himself taking the engine of his truck apart and putting it back together.

During the next few sessions, I get Carl's "blueprint."

"I need to know you. If you were a building, what you've initially told me would be the outside of the building. If something were amiss inside the building, I would have to check every electrical socket, the heating system, etc. Knowing you inside and out will expedite our work together. It will give me a deeper understanding of you up front."

Purposeful Destiny

In one blueprint question, I ask Carl to describe each parent, as if they were not his parents but individuals he knew over a span of time. I assure him the intent is not to "bash" his parents but to discover his introjects. I explain introjection happens when we internalize attributes from each of our parents.

"For example, my father was denied a high school education by my grandfather, so he compensated by continually setting high goals for himself. He passed the test to become an insurance agent, one of the few who did so without a high school diploma. He then went on to pass another test to become a real estate agent and so on, always raising the bar higher for himself. He was highly successful. My father was proud of his achievements and told us these stories during my childhood. When I went to therapy, my therapist asked me when I was going to stop attempting to conquer the world. He pointed out the introjects I got from my father's constant studying and striving against the limited expectations his dad had of him."

Carl responds with, "I'm not sure I can do this right."

"There is no right way, Carl. There is nothing to get wrong. These are just your description of your parents."

"Okay. My father's name is Tony. Everybody likes Tony. He is always helping others; he is always volunteering—he is a volunteer fireman, a Boy Scout leader, a helpful odd job guy. If you need your roof worked on, Tony will help you. If you're building a deck, Tony will be there. He is very kind and loves to be around people. He hates any kind of confrontation. If you try to get in an argument with him, he'll just walk away."

"Good job. Are you ready to move on to your mother?"

"Sure. Her name is Irene, and Irene does not like to complain—I mean, she really hates complaining. When our dog Jet died—the dog that followed my mother everywhere she went—everyone knew that she was devastated. But what did she say when any of us tried to talk to her about it? 'Oh well. Dogs just don't live as long as we do.' My mom is a complete homebody. She loves to cook and make sweaters. I think she wanted another baby. But my father thought five were enough. I always thought that's why we got Jet. Sometimes at the supper table she would announce who was pregnant in the neighborhood and then say how old they were, which was usually around her age."

"Is she quiet—reserved?"

"She is kind of shy and loves to read."

"Are you ready to move on?"

"Yes."

"Carl, if I could have been a fly on the wall in your home and no one squished me with a flyswatter, what atmosphere would I have soaked up from your early years up to about age ten? Knowing that will give me an impression of what was stressed in your home."

"Well, it was a fight for the mashed potatoes. My brothers and I would try to beat each other to them. Is this really what you want?"

"You're doing fine. What I want is exactly what comes to your mind. Besides, who wouldn't want mashed potatoes?"

"Um," Carl continues, "everything was very Catholic. Grace before meals, novenas and rosaries, and you had to be near death to miss Mass on Sunday."

———※———

When Carl returns for his next session, he walks to the couch and takes his place at the end. His eyes look bright, and he says: "I've been thinking about my parents. Don't get me wrong, they were wonderful."

"I'm sure they are, but again, I asked you to describe them because it helps me help you." He tells me he appreciates his father's generosity toward others, but he does not want to do as much for others as his father does. I ask him why that is.

"I feel sorry for my mother. I think she might feel lonely."

"But she doesn't like to complain."

"Yeah, but I think my father knows that she always blamed him for not wanting another child."

"It's probably hard living with someone who is silently blaming you for something."

"Maybe that's why he does so much for others and doesn't spend so much time at home," Carl muses.

"How much of doing something for others and not complaining is part of you, Carl?"

He is silent, pensive. "I don't know. I'm not sure—"

"Okay. That is okay, but can you think a bit about how much of both of those values might have been at work in your marriage with Valerie?"

Time passes as Carl stares down at the floor. He sighs, glances to the side, and looks straight at me. "I just don't get it," he says. "I said yes to everything Valerie wanted, yet she always seemed angry with me. I don't get why she wasn't happy."

"Carl, forgive the repetition, but how much of your parents' values were at work in your marriage?"

"Do you mean that I'm like my mother in that I didn't complain?"

"I don't know. Did you complain? Did you ever let Valerie know you felt lonely, that something needed to change? Did you ever tell her you felt hurt because you agreed to so many of the things she wanted and she didn't thank you? Don't get me wrong. Valerie has her bag of beans. We all do. It takes two people for a marriage to end. There is no saint, and there is no sinner."

When Carl comes for his next session, I ask him if he made a voodoo doll of me and stuck pins in it. He smiles and says he would never do that. Carl perches rather than sits on his seat at the very end of the couch. He says he has been thinking about his parents' marriage. Again, he remarks on how much his father does for others and how his mother holds on to her blame of him. We talk about this for a while, and I ask a question that's been on my mind.

"I know you have a lot of friends, Carl. Did you ever wonder if the reason you have so many, aside from the fact that you are a nice guy, is that spending time with all these friends might have been a way of avoiding intimacy with Valerie?"

Carl looks surprised and then annoyed. "Look, I agreed to everything Valerie wanted. I treated her like a damn queen."

"Do any of your friends not like you?"

"God no. I've known these guys since high school. I'm closer to them than I am to my own brothers."

"Well, do you know that John Prine song—I can't think of the title right now—but he sings something like 'if everyone liked me, I wouldn't have a point of view.'"[1]

"But everybody does like me."

"That's my point. Does everybody like you because you don't want to be blamed for anything? Maybe you don't have much of a point of view because that might offend or alienate or ask too much of anyone else."

Carl takes this in and says, "Geez, I hope not."

At the end of the session, I suggest a small strategy to test out what we have been discussing: Before he says yes to anyone, excluding his boss, he should visualize a stop sign. Then he should tell the person who is asking for something that he'll get back to them. Tell them he will have to think about what they have asked. We agree that between this session and the next he will try three times to visualize the stop sign and not immediately say yes.

At our next session, Carl tells me he thought about the stop sign, but he did not say no to anything. Maybe there was nothing to say no about, I suggest. Carl tells me there were things he could have said no to, but they felt like such small stuff. I ask him to give me an example.

"I mean, like when someone offers me a cup of coffee when I really don't want one. Why would I make a big deal out of declining it?"

"How do you feel inside when you use the words 'making a big deal'?"

"Like, what's the point? Nobody is going to die if I accept a cup of coffee that I really don't want."

"How do you feel?"

"I just told you."

"Tell me again."

"Why make waves over a cup of coffee?"

"Because all those cups of coffee add up to a gigantic urn! Look, are you familiar with phyllo dough?"

"I think so. First it's coffee; now it's dough. Are you opening a pastry shop?" he jokes.

We both laugh.

"Well, phyllo dough is very thin. If you were to watch a Greek pastry being made, you'd think a single layer of phyllo dough inconsequential. But layer upon layer, it forms a structure. Saying no to a cup of coffee you really don't want is like one layer of phyllo dough."

Carl expresses a fear of becoming a selfish person. He's afraid of becoming hardhearted. I assure him he has had way too much practice the other way. What he might consider rude, most people would consider an opinion.

"So you're saying I'm a people pleaser?"

"Yes."

"What's wrong with that?"

"You tell me. And take your time."

Minutes tick by. Carl's eyes focus on the pattern in the rug. Finally, he looks up from the rug and says, "It's not honest."

"And?"

"That's all that's coming up now."

"People who spend most of their time doing what someone else wants them to do and rarely what they want to do are often very angry people."

Carl is silent. He is looking down at the rug, and his forefinger is gently massaging his thumb. He slowly lifts his head up and says:

"My mother was angry. I was angry with Valerie. I felt I couldn't please her." Tears are in his eyes.

I hand him a tissue. Carl's foundation is being shaken. I think of the times I have recognized a slam dunk from God, sometimes soon enough to effect a change either with a client or within my personal life. I remember that I often felt God had punched me in the stomach or shaken me up so that I would follow His guidance. It is like when I was a child and played blind man's bluff. When it was my turn to be the blind man, my friends made sure I got spun around enough times that I would be dizzy and staggering before I headed off—unsure of my footing, hoping I would reach someone else to tag. There were plenty of times I took the blindfold off and just walked back the safe, known road home. Sometimes I left the blindfold on and tolerated the experience of being guided in a different direction.

Purposeful Destiny

I am hoping Carl will go in a different direction. I am hoping that this time he will take the unfamiliar route home.

———∿∘◦⟊⦿⟋∘◦∿———

When I next meet with Carl, I am thrilled that during the interim weeks he has been trying to travel down a new path and not attempting to please everyone. In fact, he is trying to consult himself, take the measure of his own desires, and be more authentic. One of his examples happened when he was seated at lunch with a coworker who talks a lot and he was able to tell his coworker that sometimes he needs quiet. He actually allowed himself to sit at another table. Another example is that he has the reputation of being the guy who can stay later if someone else needs to leave early and have someone cover the shift. He has managed to say he cannot cover on those occasions. He confesses that it was terrifying for him to do these things. But his clear eyes and slight smile reveal that he is proud of himself.

"That is one of the things I like about you, Carl. You try. Some people think all the work in therapy is done in an hour. It's not. I am like a music teacher. I hand out the sheet music. The people who come here have to want to practice. If they don't, I tell them their wasting their time and money."

Carl shows up the next session looking like he cannot wait to tell me something.

"What's up?" I ask.

"I realized that Valerie and I had something in common. Neither of us liked conflict. But we never said that to each other. I mean, should we have said, as you say, that we don't like to ruffle feathers? We should have. We *should* have. God, I hate coming here."

Tears stream down his face. He grabs a tissue. He takes a breath between sobs and goes on. "It's just that it never seems to end. It's like I'm caught in a cesspool. I keep finding out how I did everything ass backward. It just keeps sucking me down."

"First of all, all of us do everything ass backward. That is the way of growth. I don't know anyone who likes to see themselves before, meaning before they became aware of what they had to become aware of. Remember the dot? And remember that we can glance back, but we shouldn't stare back?"

Carl responds with a quirky, unhappy smile, and I remind him that change is not easy. At least he has been stating his preferences recently.

"Yeah, but is it going to take me thirty-three years before I can say 'Let's agree out loud that we both hate conflict?'"

"Knowing you, I'll bet you'll have it licked by thirty-two and a half. Come on, Carl, you're changing. My God, remember how you used to apologize all the time? Now you don't."

Moments of silence pass and Carl says, "You said, 'My God.'"

"So?"

"Why is God so cruel?"

"Cruel? You've got to expand on that one."

"Well, He seems to want me to hurt. When Valerie and I were married, I kept praying for our relationship to get better. I waited and waited for things to get better. He never answered my prayers. He never even knocked on my door."

"I don't agree. Every time you got angry with Valerie because you were afraid to tell her how you felt and it blew up in your face, God was knocking on your door. Every time Valerie avoided you and the reality of what was going on between the both of you, God was knocking on your door."

"Well, I wish he would have knocked louder and sooner, goddamn it!"

"Don't we all. No one likes to come face-to-face with the imperfect parts of themselves. No one. I personally hate it. I was so embarrassed when God cracked me on the head and showed me what a snob I was and what fear lay beneath that front."

"What fear?" Carl asks. "I mean, never mind—none of my business."

"My fear of being rejected."

"I'm sorry ... I'm—"

"Carl, it's not the weak who come here; it's the strong."

I thought of the many times I listened to clients say, "God was cruel," or "He must have gone on vacation because these things shouldn't be happening," or "Why isn't what I need happening? Why is He ignoring me?" And I would respond by comparing the experience to being sun blind—when someone has stared at the sun for a few seconds and feels blind. I wondered if Carl might have gone "sun blind" in not being able to see the obstacles God was providing: his and Valerie's fear of conflict and their avoidance of expressing their feelings.

The next time I see Carl he tells me he has asked his godfather, Joe, if it was okay to talk to God directly. "Good, good," I say. Carl is walking to the couch when he asks, "Why are you saying good? You don't even know what he said."

"I am saying good, because talking to your godfather shows you are thinking about talking to God directly. Carl says that his godfather told him you can do that if it makes you feel better. Again, I say "good" to what Carl has just told me.

"There you go again. Is *good* the word for the day?"

"It could be, but it's only two in the afternoon."

Carl keeps moving his hands over the top of his pants. Finally, he looks up and says, "I thought I might not be worthy of speaking directly to Jesus. He was the son of God. I'm just me."

"And that means—?"

"Come on, Joan. I haven't been nailed to any cross. I haven't saved any sinners. Have some respect. I'm sorry; that didn't come out right."

"It came out great. It was an honest feeling. I don't accept the apology, because there is nothing to apologize for. But let's head to the more interesting issue: I gather you believe there is a great disparity between you and Jesus?"

Carl almost jumps up from the couch. He says, "My God, My God. You're unbelievable. Of course there is a huge disparity—*He's the son of God. I'm not!*" Some seconds go by as Carl looks away. Then he looks up and asks, "Why am I shouting?"

"Because you're angry, and you can't believe how stupid I am. Does it feel good to be able to yell at me?"

Carl laughs. "Yeah, it does, but you're a therapist. I can't yell at regular people like that."

"Carl, I am just a person who happens to be a therapist. You simply raised your voice, and I can certainly handle that decibel level. Probably just about everyone else can too, except maybe your boss."

I go back to the Carl/Jesus disparity. Carl does a fake moan about what there could possibly be that I don't get. I tell him I believe we are all sons and daughters of God, when Carl interrupts me.

"Yeah, but when was the last time you were nailed to a cross?"

"Do you want to know the last time or all the times up until today?"

He thinks I am being sarcastic, making fun of him. I assure him I am not. I emphasize that it is *my* belief, but I truly believe that God sent Jesus to all of us. Jesus' crucifixion was God's way of showing us that, like Jesus, we could come through excruciating pain. Like Jesus, we will resurrect ourselves. We will move through suffering to a new awakening. Every disaster presents an opportunity. I told him the last time I was "nailed to the cross" was when I drove myself to the emergency room, after being unable to walk to the corner, and was told I had a huge tumor that was probably cancerous and would be operated on the next day. I practiced taking my last breaths. Obviously, I made it through. Carl is riveted to his seat.

"I'm sorry I was sarcastic."

"There you go again apologizing. I feel you are being very authentic today. Your words, tone of voice, even your expressions are not filtered."

"Yeah. Is that okay?"

"No, I just lied."

"But suppose I offend somebody?"

"My hunch is you think it's either/or. Either you're excessively polite to the point of having no opinion, or you think you're a brute."

"I do. I'm becoming a monster."

"No, you're becoming authentic."

When Carl comes back for his next session, he tells me he has had another conversation with his godfather, Joe, who told him Jesus suffered crucifixion to take away the sins of humankind, but he also agreed that Jesus died on the cross to show us we would survive hard times.

"He died for our sins," Carl says. "I treated Valerie so badly."

"Carl, did you know a better way? I believe you felt you were being generous and unselfish. From what you said, you were doing your best. Do you really think you knew a better way?"

"No, no, maybe that's how I sinned."

"Frankly, I hate the word *sin*. It is loaded with guilt. When I hear the word *sin*, I substitute something like 'away from God/

Higher Power.' I believe what you call sin is what happens when we are not in union, in sync, with Him."

"But I hate it. I hate feeling so bad. My marriage was a disaster. It was a disaster. I should not have gotten married when I did. My brother who had been so depressed waiting for a lung; you know that I told you about that. There were so many people ahead of him waiting for a donor. He was so excited I was getting married. It was the first time in a long while that I saw him smiling. I couldn't disappoint him. But I figured everything was set. I didn't want to back out."

"What was your intention?"

"I told you. I was getting married, but it must have been the wrong time."

"Carl, your intention was a good one. Your intention was not to hurt Valerie and possibly not to disappoint your brother. I didn't hear you say, 'Let's see how I can hurt Valerie.'"

"No, but that's what ended up happening."

"You're right," I agree. "But that's not what you intended to happen. You have suffered, you're suffering now, and like Jesus showed you, you will 'awaken' from this. You will come through to the other side."

"When will that happen? I feel like shit."

"Sometimes you feel so bad because you can't see a way out or imagine any other way of feeling. No options have yet come into view."

Carl's eyes grab on to that. "What options do I have? I mean, it's not like, 'Oops, I bought the wrong car; let me trade it in,' or 'Oh shit, I should have taped that plaster board better.'"

One option, I suggest, is that he consider his marriage as a lesson for him and Valerie. It might have been a way for God to show them what is not perfect about each of them. Carl looks peeved.

"You don't think God could have showed us without our marriage having to end?"

"Maybe the ending of the marriage wasn't the first time He tried to reveal that to you. Maybe it was a way of helping you realize that you couldn't have lived with Valerie for a lifetime the way the relationship was. My guess is God knew that bringing these things out now was less damaging than if you had tried to force something to work without talking about it. If He really wanted to punish you, which I don't believe, He would have left you in that hell. By learning to tell someone 'I don't like conflict,' you could be approaching healthier relationships. He could have left you in ignorance—a particular kind of hell."

Raindrops are falling against the outside windows above the couch in my office. Carl arrives with wet shoes and hair plastered to his head. "It's raining. It's raining pretty hard out there," he announces. Once he's seated at his end position on the couch, he rubs his hands over the tops of his legs and seems deep in thought. Minutes go by. He looks up and says, "Yeah, it's really raining."

"Sure is. Is there anything else you might want to tell me?"

"No."

"Okay."

More silence.

"Well, it's just that it's raining."

"Yes, but what does that mean to you? Or have you just developed a powerful interest in the weather since we last met?"

"Tears. Lots and lots of tears. There were a lot of tears when Jesus died for our sins."

"And do you think He thought everyone would be perfect from that day on?"

"How should I know? But I bet He's disappointed."

I tell him he's awfully hard on himself. Carl tells me he is a sinner. I suggest he join the club—the human club, the club that has imperfections as part of its membership dues.

"Did you ever think that painful things might happen to us so that God can show us our imperfections?"

"Why would He do that?"

"Because if we get to love ourselves imperfections and all—"

Carl interrupts me to complete my thought. "We won't be so critical of others."

"And we'll love others like God loves us. Not to the same magnitude, of course."

The atmosphere feels lighter. Carl asks how I came to feel so sure about God, and I answer that it's by wading through lots of disasters. Almost as if he is talking to himself, Carl says, "So, it's okay not to be perfect. Nobody is, and if we get that, we'll be *easier* on everybody else."

"Yes."

"So God will love us, even if we make mistakes."

"Yup. Lots of them."

"Even horrible mistakes?"

"Yup."

"Joan, do you think God really does—I mean, love us?"

"Oh, Carl, absolutely, absolutely."

Carl is beginning to accept his imperfections without feeling guilty about them. He is starting to embrace his humanity. This time when he arrives, I notice that Carl is wearing sneakers, something he's never done before. He smiles widely when I say something about them.

"I've been ... I don't know, feeling like a little load has been lifted off my shoulders. I'm not feeling as down on myself. I mean,

Purposeful Destiny

if everybody else isn't perfect either, then why should I be the only one always saying, *mea culpa, mea culpa*." Then he asks a question: "So, are you saying that if I had felt this way when I was married to Valerie, I would have loved her more?"

"I don't know if you would have loved her more. You seem to have loved her quite a lot. But I do think that if you felt about yourself then as you do now, you might have been able to understand that Valerie's words and moods were hers and that yours were yours, and you might not have been so reticent to talk about them." I ask him to imagine each life is like a movie, and each person is the director of his movie. Each day we decide whether the movie will be a horror movie, a comedy, a tragedy, or a love story. "My point is," I continue, "when Valerie was in a bad mood, she was probably directing a horror movie, and there is a good chance it had nothing to do with you."

Some time goes by, and then Carl says, "And in my movie, the sirens are blasting and the police are always after me. Valerie is the head cop. Yeah, I was always running. But I'm not running any more. No, I'm not."

"Good."

"And I hope she's not either." Carl looks lost in thought. "I guess I could never have heard myself say this before, but I was afraid of Valerie." He looks at me. "Did you hear what I said about my movie?"

"Every word."

"Which part do you think was the most important?"

"No, Carl, this is your movie. Which part is most important to you?"

"When I said Valerie was the head cop, there was no more fooling me. I was frightened of her, and I'm not running anymore. I will not run anymore."

Several months later our sessions together come to an end. Carl doesn't think he's ready. I tell him we can't meet just because we both enjoy our visits. We taper off, meeting every other week and then once a month until we say good-bye. Over the next year, he does check in for what we dub his tune-up. I am pleased to learn he has begun dating.

Then, about eight years after our last session, he calls to make an appointment. He arrives wearing the odd combination of sweats and dress shoes. He is holding a manila folder.

He sits down on the couch and spreads his arms over its back. He opened the folder and passes a photo to me. It is a wedding picture. I am thrilled for him and tell him so.

"You both look so happy."

"We are. We've been married six years. I just wanted to thank you."

I am taken aback. "Thank me? No, Carl. You did all the work. I'm just the straw; God's the juice."

"Well, we would never have gotten married if I'd still been a runner. You'd be proud of us, I think. I say what I feel now, and believe me, so does she. Thank God! You know, I never forgot those circles you drew about relationships and intimacy and how the one with the couple had to be the most important. Well, I drew those circles when I asked Carol to marry me. She just cried and said that was one of the reasons she wanted to marry me, because she believed I would put us first—not her ahead of me, like the resentful martyr I used to be—but us."

"Oh, Carl, I'm so happy for you."

"Yeah, on the way here I thought, *I hope Joan hasn't changed.* I would have been really disappointed if your office wasn't still a mess." He hands me another photograph from his folder.

"This is Judy, my daughter."

I see a beautiful little girl with blonde hair.

"Remember when you said nobody's perfect. And if we love ourselves with all our own faults, we would be able to love others, faults and all? I remember that with Judy," he says. "There is nothing like coming home and seeing her all excited, jumping around saying, 'Daddy, Daddy.'"

Passing me another photo, he goes on, "I didn't think things could get much better than this. Ralph was born nine days ago"

We just hug. There are no dry eyes in the office that day.

I miss Carl. He's a good man and fun to talk with, and now he has a great, new, hopeful life that I would be pleased to hear about periodically. I'm pretty much in awe of most of my clients—just by making the call and showing up at an office like mine means they're brave enough to go down in the trenches and willing to get dirty before they come up. I trust their intentions, I trust that some of my training will be helpful, and I trust God, the most efficient Higher Power there could ever be, to turn every one of our mistakes into something learned, something blessed.

Nash Rambler: Follow Your Dream

It is August 1989, and Bill and I have been discussing becoming parents through adoption. I never attempted pregnancy. At twelve, I told my mother: "Mom, I'm going to adopt my children because I have a lot to do."

Bill has always liked the idea of adoption. So the discussion continues: Yes or no? Is this the time to become parents?

"I have wanted to become a mother since before we even met, and I know that's my problem and not yours," I say. "So what do you think?"

"I don't know—I just don't know. I need some time."

Of course you do, I think. *You're dealing with a maniac.*

Then one day after getting home from the office, I find Bill lying on the couch in the living room, and I suggest that if we decide against becoming parents maybe we could buy a building.

"A building?" he questions.

"Yeah, we could rent offices to other therapists. And once that got going, we could buy other buildings." I get up and walk to the refrigerator, and while I'm reaching for water, Bill ends the discussion.

"Okay, Joan, I think it's time we call the lawyer."

"Do you need thirty days to think about it?"

"Nope."

"Oh, was it my talk about the buildings? Because I wouldn't want you to do this if it's not what you want."

"No, I want it, but you did have me going with the empire scheme."

My finger is pushing the number for the adoption lawyer. It feels like my finger is in an electric socket, and the excitement is zipping through my body. The attorney's wife, Barbara, answers the phone. She informs me that our baby will probably be born in Peru. She explains her husband, Joel, does many South American adoptions.

"As a matter of fact," she says, "his network in Peru includes Isabel, a social worker; Oscar, his designated liaison; Luis, his interpreter; and Antonio, his lawyer. Pretty extensive, huh?"

Stunned, I chuckle and wonder if he also has an airline connection.

Aside from the fact that we've only been married six months, I always thought there was a fear in Bill about becoming a father that he hadn't expressed. The empire scheme, the call to the lawyer, is happening the same day. I ask God to confirm that the decision we've made is the right one. Now, looking at Bill raking outside, I have no idea my Higher Power will provide not one but two responses. The first response is almost instantaneous. As I look out the large floor-to-ceiling windows in our dining room to watch Bill, I notice a piece of paper caught on Bill's rake. I watch him pull it off the rake's tine, and to my surprise, he is reading it instead of throwing it in the trash. He keeps staring at it. Then turns his head and looks at me looking at him. Bill's face is beaming. He drops the rake and rushes into the house, still holding the paper. He hugs me, smiling big, and hands me the paper. It is a scrap of wrapping paper whose design is the repeated phrase "Babies Are a Blessing, Babies Are a Blessing."

Tears stream down my face. Bill wipes them away and says, "HP knows Peru is right."

I silently say, *Thank you, God*.

Several weeks later, I receive my second response. I am taking a break in between clients when I have a sudden impulse to clean out my purse. It is a heavy bag, made of straw and leather straps. The notion to clean it out is a rare one for me. I understand that this may be a regular priority for some people, but it is unusual for me. I plunge my hand into the bag and bring up handfuls of debris. Like a little kid at the beach grabbing handfuls of the ocean floor, I keep trawling my bag.

Purposeful Destiny

In one catch pocket there is a small folded piece of copy paper. I open it and see the name *Hoey*. It is the history of the *Hoey* name, which accompanied a crest ring I had given Bill. My gaze falls on the sentence that a *Hoey* had been vice counsel of Peru in the sixteenth century. Am I amazed that an Irishman with the same last name just happened to be vice counsel of sixteenth-century Peru, where we may soon be heading? I feel so loved by my Higher Power. Only He could create such unusual circumstances.

I whisper: "I love you, HP. Thank You for Your shower of love during our adoption journey."

Several weeks go by before I realize why God has given us those two assurances. As I read the July 28, 1990, issue of the *New York Times International,* I see the following:

> In recent days suspected guerrillas from the Shining Path and Tupac Amaru organizations killed a business executive, his driver, and two body guards, burned down two large stores in Lima, killed a University official in Ayacucho and temporarily took over the northern town of Yurimaguas with unconfirmed reports of 150 people missing. Scattered clashes between police or peasant vigilante groups and suspected guerillas as well as the explosion of an incendiary device in guerrilla hands added about two dozen deaths to the toll of more than 18,000 in the 10 year insurgency.[2]

After Bill and I pore over the article, we learn that the US State Department has issued an advisory warning that it is not safe for Americans to travel to Peru. We decide to make an appointment with Marge Turcott, the gifted clairvoyant.

Marge is as glad to see us as we are to see her. Bill asks her to help us with our trip to Peru. She says: "All will go well as long as you have no fear."

I immediately think of the acronym FEAR—False Evidence (Expectations) Appearing Real. This resonates deeply with me, and I promise myself to keep it in the foremost of my mind. I affirm the practice of envisioning it. If I do not assume I will get injured in a cross fire, it will not happen. I remind myself that positive thoughts attract positive actions.

I am thinking about all this when Marge says this: "If you feel fearful, please do the following. Imagine yourselves walking along a high bluff, and something catches your eyes in the water below. You feel drawn to it. You walk down the bluff closer to the water. You see that the sparkling is Jesus Christ. He is beckoning both of you to come to Him. The pull is so great that you begin to wade into the water. You wade deeper and deeper, still being drawn to Jesus's face. He keeps beckoning you. You are frightened because the water is going to go over your heads. Just as you are sure you will drown, Jesus lifts you both up with His mighty hand." Marge is smiling big time. The wrinkles in her face are scrunched up.

Bill and I look at each other, our eyes lock, and we both agree. "Yes, we will do this."

Once in the car, Bill announces, "I'm still going to Peru. How about you?" A nanosecond passes, he looks away, and then he turns back to me with a wide smile. "HP has already let us know we're meant to go." Pointing to his heart, he says, "It feels—"

I interrupt him and say, "It feels right."

"Exactly."

Once home, we settle into our everyday lives and wait for what will happen in its own time. Four months has already passed since our visit with Marge. Bill and I are sitting in our library. It is a very small room, painted green with bookcases that reach from floor to ceiling. Bill is sitting on an old church pew we bought

Purposeful Destiny

from Oldies But Goodies, one of our favorite antique stores. The August night is hot. Our clothes are wet from a water fight earlier that day. I am about to boast that I am the winner because his clothes are more soaked than mine when I hear a heavily accented voice on the answering machine.

"Jo—an, the judge has awarded you a li—t-le boy."

"Hello, who is this?" I ask urgently.

"It is Isabel."

"Just a minute, please, Isabel."

I tell Bill that it's the Peruvian social worker, and his eyes widen.

"Well, you and Bill must come to Peru ... uh, September 16. You will be picked up at the airport. Oscar, your attorney Joel's liaison, will take you to Antonio, the lawyer handling the paperwork here. You must bring formula, diapers, and clothes for the baby. Please don't dress like the women on the television show *Dynasty*."

I hang up the phone and look at Bill. He looks like a frozen frame in a video that has been stopped for emphasis. I feel the way he looks. Then as the video moves to the next frame, we rush into each others arms and yell: "It's a boy. A boy! Yes! Yes!"

On the morning of September 16, my brother-in-law drives us to Kennedy International airport. Also in the car are my sister Marie, my mother, and lots of luggage. Nobody looks anything like the cast of *Dynasty*. It feels like the car could be powered just by the excitement contained within the people inside it. The airport is crowded, and I am relieved that we had never described the dangerous conditions in Peru to anyone in the family. Our flight number is called, we all hug, and my brother-in-law videotapes us walking to our gate with the words: "And there go the new parents."

Once we're settled in our seats, I ask Bill if the ten thousand dollars in cash is tucked down deeply in his jeans pocket. I am frightened that its loss means the adoption could not proceed. He nods and reaches for my hand. The Peruvian lawyer demanded cash for two reasons: he had been taken with checks from other couples, but more importantly, there was a bank crisis in Peru, described in the *New York Times International,* dated July 28, 1990:

> "Pensioners and state workers have lined up in vain this week to try and cash pay checks the government is unable to cover. The price of the dollar, the main hard currency used by Peru, rises and falls 20-25% a day among the money changers who crowd the streets and sidewalks, stopping cars and pedestrians." [3]

We can feel the plane descending. Bill says, "This is it."

It is after midnight when we enter Lima's airport. The floor is packed down dirt, and many people are carrying bundles tied with rope. We seem to be the only non-Peruvians waiting in the long line. Inspectors ask each person to untie and unzip packages and luggage. There is shouting, and for a second, I think I hear an explosion. Nervously, I inch closer to Bill. A woman in front of us flashes a gold-toothed smile. I smile back. We look for a sign.

Joel told us we would be picked up at the airport by a person holding a sign with our name on it. I glance down at the floor, and when I raise my head again, I see Famillia Hoey on a small piece of paper. I grab Bill's arm and point. "There it is. There it is."

The sign holder is big and burly with jet-black hair. He is wearing a brown leather bomber jacket. He motions us to follow him. The night is very dark, and the air is hot. Bill speaks what he remembers from high school Spanish, which the man seems to understand. We follow him to his car, a late fifties Nash Rambler that has no headlights—no lights period. We drive through dark streets, but I can see there are no trees. The car stops at a *pensione*. There are army trucks with soldiers holding machine guns stationed outside. I am terrified, but I remember God's two reassurances, and I recall my mother, sister, and brother-in-law saying, "There go the new parents."

It is one o'clock in the morning when we enter the *pensione*. An attractive young woman clerk speaks to our driver. He tells Bill which room is ours and that Oscar (Joel's liaison) will see us tomorrow. The driver leaves, we close the door, and we collapse into each other, only to be startled by loud knocking on our door. Before Bill opens the door, a man's voice identifies himself as Oscar. A small man with a pockmarked face walks into the room. Bill is about to speak when Oscar interrupts in English: "A picture of your son."

We see a newborn baby with a full shock of black hair and dark eyes. We both stare at the picture, and tears fill our eyes. Oscar leaves abruptly, so we get ready for bed. Before pushing the two twin beds together, we blockade the door with chairs.

In bed we look at the picture, and I feel my Higher Power's grace. Even before we knew the adoption would happen in Peru, I had visualized a baby boy. I would "see" his little body and paint it, like a paint-by-number kit, using pink and brown shades for his skin, black for his hair, and dark brown/black for his eyes. We decided to sleep with our son's picture under the pillow.

Bill looks angry, his eyes are narrower than usual, and his ready smile is not anywhere to be found. He announces that the water in the *pensione* is not reaching the third floor; in fact, it is not reaching any floor except the lobby. Bill is much more fastidious than I am, and he is mortified that he will not be able to take a shower this morning before we meet Elevenora, our future son's biological mother. I suggest that we take sponge baths in the men's and women's rooms in the lobby. A flash of panic crosses Bill's face, and he says: "Right." There is nothing like sticking your feet in a small sink as high as a ballerina's bar. I catch a glimpse of Jesus lifting me out of the water just before I am about to drown.

Feeling the great sense of relief when He saves me, I shout to Bill in the men's room next door. "I am doing Marge's visualization. Jesus just saved me."

"Good," he yells back.

In the space between when Jesus saves me and beginning the visualization again, I realize I have not been this nervous since I ran away from home as a teenager. That time I returned before my father came home. I locked myself in the bathroom, washing every article of clothing I was wearing to avoid my father, who had been drinking heavily.

When I leave the ladies room, I see Bill looking very handsome and tell him so.

"You look good too," he says.

We each take a deep breath and head to the lobby. My mind is playing out questions: Will Elevenora be angry with us for taking her son away? Will she be crying, and if so, how will I comfort her? My eyes fall on the woman in the lobby who must be Elevenora. She has long black hair and a kind face and appears to be in her midthirties. She is wearing a gray skirt, white blouse, and shoes with no heels. She exudes dignity and looks like she has been at peace with this decision for a long time. I do not want to ask her a single personal question. I do not want to be intrusive. I sense Bill feels the same.

The three of us plus our interpreter travel by bus to Mollendo, a seaport city that is two hours from Lima. While traveling, we see brown mountains, no trees, no grass—only brown earth. It is desolate. Every now and then we see a rickety unattended farm stand. From the corner of my eye, I see trees that are green and leafy and realize we have reached Mollendo. We do not see army tanks in Mollendo. We are going to court, which looks like any municipal building.

The interpreter tells us that we will be going to the judge's chambers. My stomach feels queasy. Bill's face looks angelic, but I recognize this expression as one of nervousness—Bill's way of trying to be in each second. We wait like that, second by second. When the door opens, I see a two-foot statue of baby Jesus. It is standing on a pedestal and has rosary beads around its neck. Marge Turcott's visualization comes to mind. Sitting behind a big desk is a middle-aged man, the judge. Bill and I are asked questions through the interpreter. I am afraid that the slightest mistake might jeopardize the adoption. Just then, a short, bald man enters the proceedings. The interpreter whispers that he is the court's lawyer. He begins to question Elevenora in a stern voice. "Are you giving this baby up for money?"

"No," she responds.

The lawyer's voice grows louder. "Are you selling this baby?"

I want to vomit. I want to punch his face. Elevenora's face is red, deep red. The lawyer screams this time. "Are you selling this baby?"

He is bending down to scream into her face. In my head, I am shouting, *You asshole. Stop it. Stop it—you bully.*

Finally, he backs off Elevenora and turns to Bill and me. "Did you give the mother money?" he demands.

"No," I answer. It is the truth. All the monies paid were for court procedures and for documents to be translated from Spanish to English. Elevenora's parental rights are terminated. We all leave the building.

Joan Hoey

There is a little time before the next bus heads back to the city. I walk next to Elevenora. I admire her strength and respect the love she must have for the baby she wants to spare from a life of poverty. She wants him to live in a safer country. I memorize these moments with her. I want to be able to tell our son what she is like when the time comes. When we are walking near the sea, she stops, turns, looks me straight in the face, and says in broken English, "Now he is yours."

I am so taken aback and embarrassed that I let a great moment go by. I smile gently and say softly, "Yes, yes."

As we continue to walk, Elevenora sees a wildflower. She picks it up, roots and all. Bill and I chuckle. We try to tell her at once that we do exactly the same thing at home. Bill uses his high school Spanish to tell her how we drive around the country, and when we see a field with wildflowers, we get out of the car and pull them by the roots. When Bill gets the meaning across, she smiles her biggest smile and we ours. We feel connected. Our Higher Power's grace has gently enveloped the three of us. Jesus has not let us down.

We hear gears grinding and see the bus arriving to take us back to Lima. As we board the bus, Luis, the interpreter, tells us we will be going farther south to Arequipa because it is safer. He guides Elevenora to sit with him. Bill and I whisper back and forth possible expressions of thank you to say to Elevenora when we take our leave, but none seem adequate. When we arrive in Arequipa, we look for Elevenora. We are disappointed that she and Luis have gotten off the bus and disappeared.

Purposeful Destiny

Antonio, our Peruvian lawyer, lets us know that an apartment has been secured for us. More importantly, our son will be able to stay with us. Antonio is very emphatic about the conditions and tells us not to leave the apartment or walk around the city for any reason. In answer to our questioning expressions, he explains, "Yes, we are farther south, but I repeat—do not leave the apartment. Do not walk around the city under any circumstances. Luis will take you to the apartment."

Walking us to the apartment, Luis tells us he got us a place on Jerusalem Street. I thank my Higher Power, for I feel He is winking at us. Bill and I glance at each other with knowing smiles that translate to: Can you believe HP? As I reflect on the day and the warnings, I begin to understand more fully Elevenora's decision. Peru is not the safest place for a child.

The streets are chaotic with people trying to sell anything they think someone might buy: bobby pins, hair combs, razor blades. They are aggressive in their sales strategies—not like the vendors in Manhattan who stand behind their stands with beautiful handwoven hats or handbags or even the racks of T-shirts and little tables of watches. Here mothers are selling safety pins on the sidewalks as their children, young toddlers up to school age, are lying on the sidewalks. There is no school for these kids. Everyone is shouting at the same time. Money changers are shouting that their rates are better than the banks. They are so insistent that they come within inches of people's faces. The atmosphere is so frenzied that violence seems inevitable.

We climb wooden stairs to enter our apartment. There is a bathroom without a shower or a tub, a kitchen with a hot plate for cooking, and two twin beds. Luis leaves, saying he will return with our son. The anticipation is great, and the minutes seem like hours. Finally, we hear the knock on the door. The door is opened so forcefully I am surprised it remains on its hinges, and Little

Bill is put in my arms. I feel like I have already known him for a long time. Then Bill holds him. Joy fills every molecule of air. We lie down on one of the twin beds with Little Bill between us. We begin to tell him all about the family back home, the good people in our lives, how much we love him. Later, I thought Little Bill must have wanted to shout, *Stop talking!*

We use Penelope Leach's book on parenting constantly. We haven't a clue about how to do what we are doing. Violence is still a frequent occurrence in Peru. We hear that several missionaries have been murdered farther north. We do not follow our lawyer's advice; we are too happy. Insane probably, but we feel enveloped in God's grace. We change our son's diaper on the floor of the Arequipa Cathedral. The days are sunny. We fall into a routine. I do the midnight and 2:00 a.m. feeding. Bill does the 5:00 a.m. feeding. We bathe our son in the kitchen sink. We boil his water on the hot plate.

We have been in Peru two weeks when giving Little Bill his bath one evening I look out the window to see Antonio walking in the front gate. A short, middle-aged woman is with him. At first, I think it might be Elevenora, but the woman has short hair. Elevenora's hair is long.

"Bill, Bill. Antonio is here with some woman."

"What?" he asks.

I repeat what I just said. Bill rushes out the door. I wrap the baby in a heavy towel and go outside with Bill. Antonio motions us to sit in some chairs on the lawn and speaks in English.

"You sit down. All I have now is temporary custody of your son. It will take longer for the adoption to be finalized. "Lucia," he points to the woman with the short hair, "has taken care of your son since he was born. I must ask you to return the baby until the papers are finalized."

"Excuse us, please," Bill says. "My wife and I need some time alone."

Once inside, I say, "He's not taking our son."

"Do you think I want to let him take him? Son of a bitch." Bill is punching the counter. There is just silence. Silence.

"Joan, do you remember the first time we met with Joel? He told us the adoption would be finalized quicker if we left the country—that people who stayed ended up getting jerked around."

"Yeah, but he's not holding Little Bill. I am. I'm not sure I could leave him here." Bill embraces me. We are both crying, but through his muffled sobs he says, "But don't you think it is safer for our son to be here for a shorter amount of time than a longer amount of time?"

"I can't think," I admit. "I feel like I'm going to throw up."

"Well, do you think I'm made of steel? We *have* to *think*."

We realize that we will lose our jobs if we stay longer. We are already maxed out financially. There's nothing in the bank after all this. Bill goes out and tells Antonio we need time with our baby before we leave. The lawyer says he'll be back in an hour. And he promised to have the final paperwork done in four to eight weeks.

Back inside the apartment, we sing songs to Little Bill while the tears roll down our cheeks. We do not know any lullabies, so we sing "I've Been Working on the Railroad."[4] As the time nears to go outside, we kiss each one of our son's tiny fingers, his cheeks, and his tummy.

"We'll be back," we promise. "We'll be back."

We bring him outside. As I hand him over to Antonio, my heart feels like three feet of cement have been dumped on it. Any second I feel I'm going to scream that they have to give him back. The shriek is climbing in my throat. I look at Bill. His eyes are red, and his hands are curled into tight fists. He is firm with Antonio.

"We'll be calling once a week. You must give me a number," he insists.

"Here is Luis's number. I'll tell him you will be calling," Antonio assures him. "I'll have this done in six weeks. I promise to you that I will have this done in six weeks."

Back inside we kneel in prayer. Bill prays. "HP, I seldom ask you for something, but I am asking you to keep our son safe."

While boarding the plane the next day, my mind recalls all the reassurances my Higher Power has given us. I am about to remind Bill of this when he looks at me and says: "Do you think God would have sent one piece of paper on my rake—Babies Are a Blessing—if we weren't going to be reunited?"

"Yeah, I was just going to say the same thing to you. And come on, what about *Hoey* being a vice counsel of Peru," I add. "And, hello, our apartment just happened to be on Jerusalem Street?"

"Right. And Little Bill just happened to look like the baby you visualized. I'm going to put all of this together as my screen saver."

"Absolutely."

Waiting the six weeks is excruciating. We show Polaroid pictures of our son to our families. We show them to friends and people at work. I am passing the photos to friends and read the looks in their eyes that say: "Let me get this straight, you've paid for the adoption and your son is still in Peru? You're really expecting he'll be here in six weeks? Good luck, pal." Some were just too polite to say they thought we had lost our minds. They probably read the *New York Times* article of August 16, 1990: "Baby Trail Is Leading Couples to Peru."

> The Peruvian system is not without its critics. Here babies are given to couples right after the proceedings are begun, leaving open the possibility that they will not get the child after a bond has formed. Red tape can be interminable. No centralized system or organization oversees adoptions by foreigners.[5]

We still believe in the miracles on our screen savers.

I call Luis the first week. There is a lot of static on the line, so I wasn't sure I heard him right.

"The baby is eating up a storm. In fact, they are calling him Gordo."

"Gordo?"

"Yes. I think it means fatso in English."

Finally, after six weeks, we receive a telephone call to come to Peru. The day we are leaving, October 26, 1990, I find a card on our dining room table. It is of a little boy and little girl kissing. Inside Bill has written: "I wanted to give you a little something today before all the excitement to come. God is giving us a present on your birthday, and I thank Him for you. I love you with all my heart and soul, and I know Little Bill does too."

I am overwhelmed. How thoughtful of Bill to give me this card three days before my birthday, October 29. Again, my brother-in-law, sister, and mother accompany us to the airport. It is comforting to know they too are confident that the three of us will be reunited. As we walk to the gate, they shout: "We'll be here when you return. We'll be the first faces you'll see."

When the plane arrives in Lima, we hardly notice the army tanks and soldiers. We see Luis, and his face breaks into a smile. As if he could read our minds, he tells us about Little Bill.

"The baby is at Antonio's. I will bring him to you later. We got you a place in Arequipa."

Once settled in Hotel Crisma, we wait for hours. I keep looking out the window, hoping for an arrival. Finally, I see Luis approaching with a bundle.

"Bill, Bill, he's here!" I call out.

We dash to the lobby and hold our son again. I hold him. Bill holds him. We hold him together. We do not hear a single word Luis is saying.

"Bill, Joan, please listen. You must go to the American Embassy. They will give you the final adoption papers. It is too late to go today. Adoptions are carried out on Tuesdays, so you can go tomorrow."

The next day we are standing behind a yellow line at the embassy. We are told that once our son's name is called, we can cross the line and receive the official, completed adoption papers. Each time a name is called we hold our breath. Each time Bill tells the baby we will be next. More than ten names have been called when we hear William Edward Hoey. Bill and I scream; we jump up and down; we hug our son. Bill crosses the yellow line, and we know we are now a family.

Once we're outside with our son safely in our arms, Bill turns to me. "Joan, happy birthday!" He gives me a knowing smile, and it suddenly hits me: *Oh, my God. Oh my God—He gave us our son on my birthday!*

"Yeah, I meant to mention it earlier, but I was a little distracted."

When our plane lands in New York, the first person I see as I walk down the plank is my mother. Then I spot my sister Marie and her husband, Bob, and my niece Cindy. Cindy has made a sign that reads "Welcome Home Baby Bill." Pretending to be a director, she yells, "Act one."

Bill hands out cigars to everyone. There is a picture of *all* of us with cigars in our mouths.

Once the three of us settle into our home in Connecticut, a new fear grips me. The fear is actually a question. *Am I Little Bill's authentic mother?* It scares me.

"Bill, this might sound weird, but I feel … I mean, am I Little Bill's real mother?"

Bill looks like I have taken a trip to another planet. "Joan, we did not make this baby, but you and I are his parents. If HP didn't think so, Little Bill wouldn't have entered our lives."

I am relieved, but the next day the fear takes over again. *Bam*, suddenly I find myself on my knees, calling on my deceased father to lift this fear from me. I'm crying as I call out to him, "Dad, I know you can accomplish anything. Please lift this fear from me."

The praying and tears last for several hours. I get up, and the fear is gone—completely, nada, none. *Thank you, Dad*, I think. I am amazed that he is the one I called on, because I always thought he could accomplish anything except problems dealing with emotion. I thank him again and think maybe something in heaven has changed him.

Several weeks later, as I am dressing Little Bill, I smile in gratitude and certainty that I am his mother. The day reflects my mood. The sun is shining, and when I look out the window, the sky is a beautiful blue. Today I will be taking Little Bill for his first physical. I anticipate the doctor's warm welcome. We met before our second trip to Peru, and she seemed genuinely looking forward to meeting our son. We arrive at her office. There are toys, books, building blocks, and colorful posters on the walls. A nurse ushers us into the office. There is a big smile on the doctor's face as she looks at Little Bill.

"So here is the beautiful little one," the doctor says. "Let's put him on the table and check him out. He certainly doesn't look undernourished."

"No, they called him Gordo in Peru. That means fatso."

"I'm afraid he's not going to like me after I stick him with this needle."

"No worries. I will kiss him all over and try to distract him with this shiny musical carousel."

He screams, but in minutes he is all smiles again, and the visit ends with him getting a sticker. Once home I settle Little Bill in his bouncy chair. I am talking to him when the telephone rings. It is the pediatrician, and she does not sound happy.

"Hi, Doctor, is everything all right?" I ask.

"Joan, I'm calling because your son has hepatitis B."

Not knowing exactly what that meant, I asked what we could do about it.

"Well, nothing."

"Nothing?" My heart starts to beat faster.

Hearing the fright in my voice, she says, "Joan, about 10 to 15 percent who have it recover, and we don't know exactly how or why that happens."

"My God," I gasp. "What can we expect?"

"He could develop cancer. He could live until he is forty."

I am speechless. My mind recalls all the reassurances God sent us—even the one when we discovered that all three of our birthdays fall on the same day of the week. An epiphany hits me: God has sent this baby to us so he can die in a loving environment. While these thoughts are flying across my mind, the doctor informs me that Little Bill will have to have his liver tested once a month. I hang up the phone and sob.

A half hour later, Bill comes home from work. He sees my face and asks if my mother has died.

"No, but our son might."

"What? What are you talking about?"

"The pediatrician called. She said Little Bill has hepatitis B—he could live to forty." I break down and try to tell him the rest.

Tears are rolling down his face. He holds me tightly and says, "No. HP has not sent our son to us to die—no way. Everything is going to be fine."

Later that night, I remember the words of Bette J. Eaddie, the author of *Embraced by the Light*. She wrote that every prayer in heaven is answered, even those said rotely. When she had died for several minutes and went to heaven, she saw these prayers show up like tiny pinpoints. Prayers visualized illuminated wide areas like spotlights on an opening night.[6]

I decide to practice visualization. I "paint" Little Bill's body. I see the hepatitis B as little black dots exiting his body through his hands and feet. I repeat this visualization every night. Each month we bring a happy baby to Yale New Haven Hospital to have his liver tested. He screams, and Bill and I wilt at the sound, wishing there was some way to prepare him.

I drive Little Bill for his next physical. He's happily singing along with a Raffi tape. Today is his fifteen-month checkup. Entering the office, he immediately heads for the building blocks. Once in the doctor's office, his folder containing the latest liver test is opened. She is looking at the results, does a double take, and then looks at the paper again.

"Joan, he doesn't have hepatitis B anymore," the doctor reports. "He has developed antibodies."

She is smiling widely. I feel an explosion of joy. I jump up, because I cannot stay still, and I say, "Thank you, Jesus. Oh, I have been visualizing every night for it to leave his body."

She looks at me kindly. I imagine she is wondering what I'm talking about.

Relief and gratitude are the only emotions evident in our home. It causes us to recall the visualization Marge Turgett taught us before we left for Peru. We decide to visit her. As we park the car, we see her looking out a big window and smiling at us. We thank her for the Jesus visualization she gave us. She nods and addresses Bill.

"Don't you know that you and the beautiful Joan were married in another lifetime? Joan was an Indian and you, Bill, were a woodsman. In that life, Joan died in childbirth."

Bill's expression shows no confusion. In fact, there is a strange clarity. "You know, I was ambivalent about a child in our lives, but it felt like fear—a fear I could not articulate."

He looks at me, and I take his hand and tell him I know he would have explained it if he could. Lucidity strikes me as well, for it clarifies why pregnancy had never appealed to me. We talk a bit more, and it comes to us: Peruvians are a mix of Inca Indian and European ancestry!

Gabby:
Loving Yourself First

Her raven, shoulder-length hair is in her face. Any semblance to a styled coif is gone. Gabby is wiping her tears and the residue from her nose with her sleeve. She is sitting on the edge—the very edge—of the couch with one long leg and foot anchored to the floor. Through her sobs, she says: "I'm not in bars any more, but let me tell you, the guys on dating dot-com might as well be. No … no," she sputters—"not drunk, just dorky. And Miss Beautiful here slept with one last night and not even after a long dinner. What do you think of that, Joan?" There is an emphasis on the first syllable of my name.

"I think you're terrific, smart, and lonely, and it's a big change not looking for guys in bars," I say. "But I would go for an AIDS test just to be safe."

Gabby is thirty-three and very attractive. She is an elementary school teacher. Today is our fifth session, with the previous four focusing on why she is coming to therapy and an in-depth intake. A blueprint, which includes a description of each parent's personality, the atmosphere in her home until the age of ten, and many other questions.

"An AIDS test?" Gabby asks. "I really hit bottom, but I'd be lying if I didn't say it crossed my mind." She looks over my shoulder at a tapestry behind me as if it had a message. She turns her head slightly, looks at me, looks away, and then looks back at me. In a low voice she tells me that she has been asking the Universe, God, to send her a partner. "But He mustn't hear me. And I have asked a thousand times: out loud, whispering, and even on my phone."

"Maybe He doesn't know how to text."

She chuckles, and so do I. "I believe God hears you. But imagine He saw a herd of sheep heading in a direction that ended in a cliff and if reached, they would fall to their deaths. He would slam down a wall. They would get banged up, but they would survive and go in a different direction. God, the universe, is hearing your prayers, but He wants you to go in a different direction. He is not a control freak; He only wants what is for your highest best."

"Well, my head hurts, and I want it to stop. And just how am I supposed to know which way to go, *if He is not answering me?!*"

She has moved back on the couch, and one leg is crossed over the other with one high-heeled shoe dangling.

"Gabby, bear with me and tell me again about your parents while growing up."

She does a mock groan. "But we went all over that." And then in a singsongy voice, she tells me: "My mother wanted everything perfect—I mean, not just everything in its place kind of thing, but it was her way or the highway. She is smart; I'm not taking that away from her, but I never heard her say she made a mistake."

"What was your father's reaction?"

"He and I would joke and pray a misstep would blow up in her face. Don't get me wrong—he loves her, but he is an easygoing guy."

"Gabby, part of your therapy is to discover different directions to travel. Remember, it's not the weak who come here but the strong. Between now and the next time we meet, I would like you to make a list of your mother's values: what she thinks is right and what she thinks is wrong. I would like you to do the same for your father and review each list, almost like a restaurant menu. Then make a list and choose which values you would keep from each parent and which you would discard. Also add any values that are important just to you."

"Should I have my parents sign it?" She is smiling to see if I got the ribbing.

"No, you're past junior high school. Just complete it and bring it in with you."

"Okay, teacher."

The sun is shining through my office windows, and Gabby is going through her lists. Her mother values specific cleaning products, small birds, and crystal vases; she tunes out others' opinions, including her husband's. Her father values silence, books, classical music, and church on Sundays where he sings in the choir. His most frequent response to his wife is: "Yes, dear."

I interrupt her. "Does your mother go to church with him?"

Gabby laughs a hearty laugh. "Are you kidding? She says each Sunday: 'What a total waste of time.'"

As we move to Gabby's list, her mouth looks like it is caught between a smile and a grimace. Her right hand is squeezing the area above her right knee.

"Tell me what is most important to you on your list, and take your time."

Tears begin to roll down her cheeks, and sobs shake her shoulders. "I never realized how much I hate my mother—well, not hate. I mean, how much I dislike her. But there are things I do like about her—like how clean she keeps the house." Gabby stops, looks at me, and starts laughing. "Who cares if there are no spinach stains in the sink. Uh-oh, the fashion police are after me because I'm wearing red lipstick and orange pants."

We are both laughing. "Watch out! Arrest is apparent," I say.

The laughing subsides, and she says, "I know she loves me; she tries. But *thank God I don't live there* anymore. I feel sorry for my father." She explains he does whatever his wife wants and redoes things to please her.

I ask her for an example.

"I remember one Sunday morning—I must have been about eight or nine years old—and my father and I got up before Mom," she begins. "We were mixing pancake batter—or, I should say he was letting me stir, and every now and then he'd give a good stir with the big wooden spoon. Mom came into the kitchen and shrieked about the mess on the counter from the batter. She looked in the bowl, picked it up, and dumped the 'pancakes' into the garbage. She informed my father that eggs, toast, and juice would be a healthier breakfast. He made that breakfast. I only ate it because my dad made it."

"How has this example affected your relationship with men?" I ask.

"I only choose men who like pancakes."

"Who wouldn't—but try again."

Gabby is running her fingers through her hair. She looks straight at me. "I hate coming here. What's so great about insight?" Her right hand is in the "stop" position. "Don't answer that; please don't answer that. I want to get what's inside me out, or I'll never say it—*never*. I often wished my mother was dead." Tears are running down her cheeks. "Then my father could have fun—we could have more fun together."

I move closer to her. "You're brave. That was hard—thank you."

She wants validation she is not a horrible person. I ask her to continue to look at me. I brush my left shoulder off with my right hand and brush my right shoulder with my left hand. "See, no wings."

———∿∿∘◠⨯◉⨯◠∘∿∿———

Gabby is talking before I close my office door behind her, which is unusual. "I was talking to my best friend Liz. I've known her since fifth grade, and believe me, she doesn't mess around— uh, that doesn't sound right. I mean, *she tells it straight*. I asked her to describe, especially after our last session, the men I've dated and been involved with." She suddenly stops. "Joan, isn't it hot in here?"

I get up to adjust the thermostat. "I could live on the equator." Our chuckles bounce around the room. But I also wonder if it's Gabby's reaction to her friend's words. Gabby relays Liz's description.

The profile includes men who could be bossed around, men who like to drink too much, and men who are not as smart as Gabby. We discuss the accuracy of the description. Her face clouds over; her forefinger and thumb are squeezing the bridge of her nose. She conveys that after an initial angry reaction, which resulted in not talking to Liz for a few days, she realized much of the depiction was accurate.

"Well, I asked her, didn't I? I knew it wasn't going to be pretty." She laughs a deep, throaty chuckle that sounds cynical. "Joan, do you really believe God slams us into a wall so we'll change? I mean, really?"

"No," I lied.

"Boy, I really choose them."

"You sure do. But, yes, I absolutely believe God slams us with every type of obstacle until we recognize them and go in a different direction. Haven't you noticed all the bumps on my forehead?"

"I thought it was acne."

We are both laughing hard and pointing at each other, saying; "You," and "No, you."

"Look, here's a once-upon-a-time parable," I begin. "A man was walking down a street while texting and fell into a hole. He cursed, picked up his phone, and got back on the pavement. The next day while walking to work on the same street and answering a text, he fell into the hole again. He cursed himself again, rubbed his shins, and promised himself tomorrow he would avoid the hole and would not use his phone. The next day he remembered he was going to avoid the hole. *I'll leap over it, and no phone*, he thought to himself. As he approached the hole, he stretched his legs and extended his foot to do the leap. However, he fell in the hole again because he miscalculated. He thought, *And I didn't use the phone.* Later, at home while eating his dinner, a thought came to him. *I don't have to walk down that street. I can go a different way.* The next morning he walked down a different street, he didn't fall, and he texted all the way until he reached work."

"Wow, he had all the lights on in his shed—like, not. Like, *hello.* How stupid. The guy was stupid."

"Aren't we all?"

"Not you, Joan."

"Of course me."

"You're not freaking serious." She smiles a crooked, skeptical grin. Seconds pass. The minute hand on the clock behind her reaches twelve again when she says, "What kind of God, who supposedly loves us, makes us wait? Why doesn't he show us the first time?" She extends her middle fingers in the air.

"Because He knows you can't bake a cake at four hundred degrees. It will disintegrate. Most of us don't want to change. It's like reverse breathing: exhale first, then inhale. It takes too much energy to remember the 'new' way."

"It's scary."

"Yup," I agree. "Look, here's another once-upon-a-time—"

"I think you must have taken a giant mother, of a once-upon-a-time pill."

We are laughing hard, very hard. "Yeah, and it was ugly with tiny bumps on it."

Gabby is laughing so hard she is imitating me by slapping her thigh as the laughter ensues.

"Okay, no stories. I think—"

"No, no, there is no way I'm *not* hearing that story. No way."

"Okay," I continue. "A man is seated on the second floor of his house because there is a flood in his village and the water has filled the first floor. He prays to God to rescue him. As he is praying, a neighbor in a pickup truck yells for him to get in the truck. The man refuses and says God will save him. Hours go by; the water has reached all the rooms in the house. The man has had to climb out onto his roof. Some people come by in a boat yelling to him to get in so he can be taken to safe ground. He repeats what he told his neighbor: God will save him. Shivering in the dark, on his roof, a helicopter spots him. The pilot offers to take him to a secure place, but the man repeats his belief. After he drowns and is in heaven, he asks God: 'Why didn't you save me? I prayed and prayed.' God said, 'I sent you a pickup truck, a boat, and a helicopter, and you refused them all.'"

Tears are in Gabby's eyes. "It makes me think of my father. I have always felt he was drowning in our house, and although I didn't use the word *rescue*, that wish was in my heart."

I suggest that similar to the man in the story, perhaps her father did not recognize God's help, did not want it, or thought prayer would create a change that did not necessitate his changing. The possibility that met with the most resistance from Gabby was that her father was "happy" in his marriage. As our hour is ending, I suggest she try not to think of her dad as a victim.

———

At our next session, Gabby begins by telling me she agrees with a lot of what I say but cannot imagine her father as anything but a victim. "I mean, how would you like to live with someone you always had to please?"

We are four minutes into the hour. "It would be difficult unless that was what I wanted."

Gabby has inched to the edge of the couch and informs me, with an edged tone, "You'll have to expand on that one."

"There are different forms of happiness beside the 'romantic' images music, some movies, and often novels present. Have you ever known a couple who argues more times than not? And not over serious matters?"

Gabby's determined expression remains. "Oh yeah, believe me, I know a few."

"Have you ever wondered why they stay together?"

"Because of the kids or because of money?"

"Maybe. Those are certainly common reasons. But sometimes a couple argues consistently because it fulfills the need of distance. Not everyone wants the same level of intimacy. Arguing puts the needed space between them. Look, maybe your dad's constant agreement with your mom's wishes provides the distance he needs."

Gabby is looking down at the rug's design. Her fisted hands uncurl and curl again. She looks up and says in a whisper, "I don't have to rescue my father."

"No, you don't."

"I've lived most of my life believing he's been miserable with Mom, I get what you're saying, but I'm not sure I can sustain it. I'm afraid I'll keep texting and falling in the hole."

"Of course you will—like all of us. It takes time for any new thought to feel comfortable."

Gabby is smiling an impish smile. "Joan, I just got slammed into one of God's walls."

We high-five, and I ask her to try to think the "new" way about her father five times between now and the next time we meet.

"Joan, every time I tried to think of my dad being 'happy' in his marriage, I thought, *This is ridiculous.* I mean, I was over at their house for dinner Sunday, and he looked miserable. She's always on him."

"Why does this concern you so much?"

Gabby shouts, "*What are you—crazy? Because he's my father, that's why!* I'm sorry I'm yelling. I just don't get you sometimes."

"It's your hour. You can yell as much as you want. But tell me, aside from him being your father, why does this concern you so much?"

She sniffs three times quickly with her chin moving up. Her frustration bounces around the room. I hear trucks rumbling outside my office. Softly, she says, "I don't know. The only thing that's coming up is because *He's* my father."

"Remember, you said last time that you don't have to rescue your father?"

"Yeah, but I wasn't in the same room with him."

"Right."

We discuss her father, his high intelligence, and his ability to problem solve at the university where he is cochair of a department. Gabby relays her feeling that she has to protect him. She muses that this is a carryover from childhood. I suggest she does not have to keep it. She chortles her cynical chuckle and fears leaving him in a messy situation. I assure her there is nothing to fear and more than likely her parents made an implicit agreement long ago how their relationship would work. Gabby nods, taking this in. I gently remind her that her goal in therapy is to find a life partner.

She looks at me with sad eyes. "Do you truly believe God is loving?"

"Oh, Gabby, I truly do. He loves your parents. He knows their needs. I think of Him as a huge electric plant like the United Illuminating Co. in Connecticut. He sees the whole territory, and I think of us as small, decorative Christmas lights. Our knowledge, in comparison, is ridiculously limited."

"So, if I leave my parents, I will have a better chance at a relationship."

I slap her high five and remind her she is very smart. I ask her between now and the next time we meet to gather nine sheets of paper and on each ask: How has my relationship with my parents affected my relationship with men? And then answer the question.

"Do this nine times, and do not do it hurriedly," I suggest.

The office phone rings, and I hear Gabby's voice on the answering machine. I pick it up and hear her say that she is cancelling her appointment tomorrow. She tells me she is going to California and will call me when she gets back. I feel sad, not sure she will make another appointment. I know this often happens when a change is about to take place. I say a prayer that God will do what is for her highest best. Several weeks pass, and Gabby calls to make an appointment. The following week I open the door to my waiting room and see a not tanned Gabby. Her head is down, and she is pulling each finger to crack a knuckle.

She looks up at me. "I didn't go to California. I lied."

"Oh my! You better go to confession! Seriously, I am so glad you are here."

She walks into the office and takes her usual seat on the couch. She needs reassurance that I am not angry with her.

"Take me through your feelings since we last met."

"Well, I did the nine questions, and I got angry and tore them up. First I was angry with you and had actually decided not to come back. Of course, I called Liz, and she told me I was probably ticked off at you because what I had come up with was true, and I didn't like it. That is when I cancelled, and I also took days off from work. I just took long walks by the water; the water always calms me. And then I allowed the awful truth to come up: that I'd been praying to God to rescue me without me changing, like the guy on the roof." Tears are running past her chin, and she is twisting her fingers. "I realized I wanted to be the 'leader' with my dad, and I stayed away from guys who had strong opinions because I wasn't going to be 'bossed' around like I thought my dad had been. What a mess. I never realized I was such a baby."

"Look, we're all babies. It's one of the reasons I don't like the word *grown-up*. It connotes that at some point we're finished emotionally growing, and to me, that would be death. I prefer *human beings*, because, hopefully, we'll keep evolving."

"Yeah, but is it going to hurt this much?"

"I think each spurt of growth is different. Look, at one point in my life I thought to 'love' someone I had to first be physically attracted to him. I got so tired of people asking me: 'Why isn't an attractive woman like you married with children?' My response was because I hated children. Of course, that was not true."

"No way. Did you really? Wait ... wait, you probably did. But you found someone—oh, I'm sorry ... I—"

"Don't apologize. I found more of me, and then shortly after, my husband and I met. We didn't particularly think the other was the man/woman of our dreams physically. We loved the inside first, and then the outside became irresistible. Don't get me wrong; I am not against physical attraction. But to get back to your wondering if every growth spurt is going to hurt this much—I don't think so. Look, what you just discovered is big."

"Yeah, you can say that again."

"What you just discovered is big."

Smiling, she says, "I knew you were going to do that."

And we both say in unison: "Redundancy communicates."

"Look, what you realized is like having been burned deeply."

"It means breaking up with my dad." The sobs are loud and long. Minutes go by, and the sobs get softer and lower. As I hand her another bunch of tissues, she looks up and says, "You're going to have to put plastic covering on this couch for your next person."

"Don't worry. I've got a wet vac."

Over the next six weeks, we discuss a more adult-to-adult relationship with her father and, of course, her mother. Often repeated is the cliché "hindsight is twenty-twenty" and the notion that one can look back but does not have to stare back, for it can create anxious feelings. Slowly, Gabby is becoming her own "parent," directing herself to do activities that she likes and not needing someone to accompany her if she wants to go to the movies, etc. She decides to stop dating for a while until she feels more centered. She claims my statement: "Hungry people make poor shoppers" is one of her affirmations. She has good insight and relays during one session that she realizes her prior sexual life was a release from her bind with her father.

"I know I slept with almost complete strangers because I was so frustrated with my father and mother. I needed to be cuddled and soothed, even if they were lies." She is looking at me as if she expects me to reprimand her.

"Of course you needed to be cuddled and soothed; you were carrying a big burden."

"That's all you're going to say?" She is turning her face away from me. I see her profile.

"Gabby, you look disappointed that I'm not yelling at you."

Softly, she asks me if I would.

"Gabby, remember you are now your own parent. If you want a part of you to be scolded, then do it. I'd like to hear it."

A squirrel is scampering across the lawn as I gaze out one of my office windows. She tells me she can't do it now. I assure her I hardly expected her to do it today.

Suddenly, she is standing in front of one of the chairs and sternly saying, "Look, little miss sunshine, you're not a ho. You're not some freaking dead fish that's going to lay down for everyone. Do you hear me? *Do you hear me?!* The next time masturbate I will tell you I love you, I love you, I love you."

She looks at me rushes into my arms, and I whisper, "You are loved; you are loved." Moments later, she has taken her usual place on the couch.

She asks, "Was that right? Did I do that right? I don't want to sound like my mother."

"Did it feel right to you?"

Softly, she answers, "Yes."

"Because it felt like it came straight from your heart."

"It did. I wish my mother would have talked to me like that—I mean … I mean, straight from her heart. She had no trouble speaking to Fantastic, her favorite cleaning product, like that: 'Oh, this Fantastic is sooo good,' as she is pressing her cheek against the bottle. I know what you're going to say: 'You can look back, but you don't have to stare back.'"

"Yup. And you're a great mother to that daughter part of you. You showed her you loved her by being so upset. Now, I wouldn't suggest you beat her."

Gabby smiles and takes a deep breath. She wonders how she will do this outside my office.

"Well, I wouldn't yell out loud to that part of yourself walking down the street, or they'll take you away in a big net."

She chuckles. I relay she can parent herself with her inside voice. She asks if I parent myself. I assure her I do.

Gabby is chuckling as I turn down the heat in my office. She asks me if I've always liked this much heat. I tell her I was the kid who wore sweaters in the summers while climbing trees. We chat about tree climbing, when she relays she read a magazine article that endorsed taking time off from dating. She is smiling, proud of herself. Before I respond, she informs me a friend (not Liz) asked her if she would go on a blind date with her cousin. I inquire about her answer. She puts up her hand, letting me know there is more to tell me.

"Then, Joan, a week later a college friend calls out of nowhere asking me if I was available. Wait, wait, you're not going to believe this. Today a colleague told me she had a perfect guy for me and asked if I was interested."

Smiling, I relay how it reminds me of how I got to be a clinical hypnotherapist. I clarify that there is no transition. Gabby looks puzzled. I imitate her "stop" position. She nods.

"One day while looking through my mail I saw an advertisement for clinical training in hypnosis. I threw it away. Several weeks later another advertisement for training in hypnotherapy came. Again, it got thrown away. Driving home one night, letting the day roll off me, I walked into our dining room, and there, spread out on the table, was a double-page article on clinical hypnotherapy in *NASW*, our social worker magazine. My husband saw my surprised look, because neither of us read it at home, and said, 'I thought this might be interesting to you.'"

Gabby asks, "What did you think?" Her arms are extended toward me.

I impart that I knew the Universe was directing me to get my clinical hypnosis certification. I got it, and it's helped many clients. Gabby gets up and slowly walks back and forth in front of the couch, giggling. She looks at me and flashes her biggest smile.

"You know, the first thing I was going to tell you today is that I feel fuller, less empty and frightened inside. And, yes, this feeling has been happening a little bit at a time—like drops from an eye dropper. I've sort of felt I was on the brim, as you say, of something happening."

"I think you are."

"What do you think it is?"

"I think you know what it is and can tell me when you're ready. I don't mind you walking up and down in front of the couch."

She smiles and lightly touches her hand to her heart and says, "I'm ready to date. Remember a long time ago when I asked you: 'But how do we know what direction God wants us to take?'"

"I sure do."

"Well, it's like your story about the hypnosis. Three different people have mentioned me dating. And, Joan, that just happened to coincide with a growing feeling of—I'm afraid to say it—confidence. C'mon that is no accident. The UI is working."

"Give that beautiful lady the Porsche behind door three."

Buoyant molecules are floating in the air. Gabby has been sitting comfortably on the couch with her back relaxing into the pillow. She tells me she is not going to be Velcro this time. She is not going to stick to just anyone.

"Good, I am proud of you."

Gabby is looking very pretty today, and I tell her.

"Oh, you don't think I have cottage cheese legs?"

My eyes telegraph question marks.

"Okay." She is giggling. "Okay, yesterday after school I ran into get a pizza. I left my coat in the car. No sooner am I at the register, when a guy from my old neighborhood recognizes me.

After giving me the once-over, he says: 'You have cottage cheese legs.'"

"How catchy. How endearing."

She relays that at another time she would have flipped him the bird. But she pretended not to hear him, did not look at him (even after he said he was only razzing her), and walked out.

"But, Joan, before, I would have thought: *Oh my God. Do I?* I would have gone home and stood in front of the mirror checking my legs out. But instead I knew I'd never go out with someone like him."

"And so bright too!"

A small frown crosses Gabby's face. She shares her anxiety about rejecting people. I stress that when she's serious about dating it is not important if they like her. It's important if she likes them. I convey an instance when, although I liked a particular fellow who liked me very much, I had to tell him we would not be walking off into the sunset together. She wants to know exactly what I said. A few seconds go by, and she assures me I don't have to tell her. Gabby's eyes brighten as I begin the story.

"I said, 'Hugh, I like you very much. But this is not going to be a romance. If you still would like to go to the movies or concerts together from time to time, I'd like that. But I have to be straight with you.'"

Gabby wants to know if I felt guilty. I tell her I did not; I felt honest.

"But how did you know he was not the one?"

"Because I thought long and hard about what I wanted in a life mate, and he did not have the characteristics important to me. Look, imagine you were choosing a business partner for an enterprise you dreamed of and are now ready to launch. Wouldn't specific traits come to mind?"

"Yeah, but it sounds unromantic."

"Good. Or, to put it another way, how would you feel about someone who has your back?"

"I'd feel safe."

"Gabby, think about the characteristics *you* want, because you're launching an enterprise you're ready for and have dreamed of."

Gabby comes in with a large coffee for me. She lets me know she put two packets of sugar in it and half-and-half. Thanking her, I inform her I am a diabetic, and although I would love to drink it, I would probably end up in outer space. We look at each other mischievously and remark such an experience might be fun. She then shyly hands me a sheet of paper. I am in the process of handing it back for her to read aloud to capture her tone of voice, her expressions, and her gestures. She pleads with me to glance at the list on the paper. Before returning it to her, I realize it is an inventory of male physical characteristics.

She looks at me and says, "It just seemed too unromantic not to do it this way." I assure her my job is not to control her life. Relaxing more, she reads the list. "He must have nice abs; he cannot be unmuscular, and I like muscles. Blond hair is preferred." She is still smiling when she finishes the list, and her nonverbal cues and her voice have remained animated. She inquires about my thoughts. I relay that it is good to see her happy. Her affect notches down and she says, "I passed the list by my married sister."

"And?"

"She said, 'What are you going to do when he has a potbelly and has gone bald? My butt looks like a minivan, and there are gray streaks in my hair.'"

I inquire if her sister is happily married.

Gabby's answer is quick: "Absolutely. Maureen asked me: 'Did I look like that when I got married? You were one of my bridesmaids.'"

Gabby tells me it took a few ocean hours to calm her. But once home, she found her bridesmaid present—a small wedding album. She relayed that at first glance there was no comparison and adds quickly that she did not expect one, but it made her feel like the wax candy doll, where the blue liquid had only reached the feet.

"Why?" I ask.

"When making the list, I was only thinking of now and not a lifetime."

"It doesn't mean whomever you marry will become bald and have a potbelly. Or that your rear end will resemble a bus."

"No, it didn't hit me that it would be for a lifetime."

"Look, walking off into the sunset sounds so romantic. It implies from that day there will be no struggles, no problems. How many people think about 'after'?"

"I haven't." She looks to the side, runs her fingers through her hair, sighs a deep sigh, and tells me she does not know if she is meant for the long haul.

"Good."

"Good?"

"Yes, now you're thinking past Hollywood."

Gabby is holding a coffee and bottled water. She is telling me she remembered about the no sugar but did not know if diabetics were allowed to have caffeine. I assured her I could have caffeine but preferred not to have more than my morning cup and a half of coffee. As she is handing over the water, I thank her but remind her she does not have to bring me something every time she wants to drink coffee during a session. She makes an exaggerated sad expression and informs me she will never do it again. Chuckling, I convey I would drink several bottles of water not to witness *that* face. As I am twisting the cap off the water bottle and Gabby is sipping her coffee, she asks me what I think the "long haul" means.

"What does it mean to you?"

Her answer is quick. "Boredom. It just seems it would be awfully boring living with the same person day in and day out."

"You're right. It's not for everyone."

"Yeah, but there are some people whom it is right for. You're going to love this: like my parents." She looks at me and chides me for beaming. I impart I can beam at my own discretion.

Silence ensues, and then, looking earnestly at me, she asks, "What makes it work for some people?"

"Knowing commitment is an everyday phenomenon."

"Yeah, but doesn't everyone know that? You don't sleep with other people."

"I believe it's much more than that—it's knowing and wanting to devote energy to the relationship. It's not mistaking espousal love for parental love. Some of us knew we just had to 'be there,' and our parents would love us. Look, when you're in the classroom, do you say: 'Oh, I won't teach today.' You might for a day or two, but you couldn't do that for several weeks; you would get fired. Or let's say you decided to take a break from being your cat's keeper but didn't get a cat sitter—"

"She'd be dead."

"Yup."

"You're saying it takes everyday caring, everyday caring."

Gabby's body is very still. She is looking past me. "I don't know if I can do that."

"You already know how to do it in smaller arenas—one day at a time. Did you love some of your students the first day like you do now?"

"God, no. But—p"

"Gabby, you don't have to decide today if you want a committed relationship—"

"God will let me know." A smile is forming on her face. "Joan, you better get ready to see lots of bumps!"

She gets up, and as she walks to the door, she turns and gives me a hug.

Several months have passed, and I feel Gabby is ready to come twice a month. She has been dating and has not been a "hungry shopper." She surprises me the next time we meet by handing me a list of inner qualities she would like in a partner in case the "long haul" becomes a reality. While holding the list, I inquire if this means she has a candidate and is feeling less ambivalent about a life partner.

She giggles embarrassingly, looks down, and slowly picks her head up. "The Universe/God will let me know," she says.

We chat about the personality characteristics on her list, which include honesty, trustfulness, intelligence, and a belief in a Higher Power. I am feeling happy and sad. Happy because Gabby is so healthy and sad because I know our work has ended.

Gabby picks up on my feelings. "Joan, you look kind of sad. I'm not used to seeing you with a gloomy face."

"This is the face each client sees when her work is finished."

"I'm not finished."

Tears well up in her eyes as well as mine. I suggest that we taper off, seeing each other once a month, then every six weeks, and finally in three months. She tells me she had the feeling this was going to happen soon, but she liked "seeing" me. The session ends with two strong hugs and each of us thanking the other.

Several months after our last scheduled meeting, Gabby telephones me. "Joan, I have found someone I really like. He's smart, trustworthy, and spiritual. And you're going to love this—we met on a dot-com dating service. And he and I agree to take this—"

We both shout: "One day at a time!"

No Siblings Knocked Down Flat: The Road Doesn't End, Take the Turn

Purposeful Destiny

It is 1993. Relatives and friends are stifling giggles behind closed doors of a room rented off of Dwight Chapel on the Yale campus. I am excited and trying to look calm, usual. I cannot wait for Bill to open the door and for everyone to yell "surprise."

His hand is on the door. He opens it, and loud shouts of "surprise" ring in our ears. He looks at me and says, "Oh my God."

The party is for his promotion to vice president of a drug and alcohol facility. I welcome everyone and say, "Nine years ago, when Bill was in early recovery and a volunteer at an alcohol and drug agency, he said, 'Someday I am going to be an executive at a drug and alcohol facility.' Well, that day has come."

Everyone cheers and claps. The party is a success.

Several weeks later, after a trip to Washington, DC, that the three of us took for my training in clinical hypnotherapy, Bill's job was eliminated. We got home late from DC. It was even later before Bill came to bed because we were getting our son settled. I woke up the next morning to the phone ringing. Picking up the receiver, I hear Bill's voice on the other end of the line.

I say, "Bill, you sound real tired."

"I am tired. But, Joan, my job has been eliminated."

"What? I mean, why?"

"It all happened within ten minutes," he says. "They said they had to scale back, and my job was eliminated."

"Oh, I'm so sorry. I'm so sorry. Don't worry."

"I'm trying not to. HP must have a plan," Bill says. "But, Joan, I don't know about the second adoption now."

"I know, I know."

Driving to DC to get my clinical hypnosis certification, I am keeping Bill J company in the backseat. He is three years old, and he wants to be called Bill J rather than junior, because Little Bill is a baby name. We are singing songs. Actually, Bill J is singing his favorite Raffi song, "Must Be Santa."[7]

He says, "Mommy, you play the drums, and *I'll* sing."

He sings and I drum for more than two hours. Finally, I say, "I'm going to sit up front with Daddy." As I am climbing into the front seat, he begins begging me to keep up the "Must Be Santa" gig when his father says: "Now, Bill J, it's getting late. We are all going to close our eyes and rest."

There is a momentary pause, and we hear, "You better not close your eyes, Daddy. You're driving."

Bill and I look at each other and hold in the giggles. I wait until Bill J falls asleep before I say: "Bill J said he wanted a sister."

"Really? When?" Bill questions.

"About a week ago. I feel guilty he doesn't have a sister, as he says, 'for later.'"

"But then, Joan, if he has a sister or brother, it doesn't mean they'll be close like you and Marie."

"I know, but who will he have after we're gone?"

"He'll have his own wife and his own children."

"Look, I just wanted to tell you what he said and my feelings."

"I'm not against it. I—"

"Well, I wouldn't want you to agree to another child if it was something you didn't really want; it's not like me saying, 'Okay, I'll go to a football game because I know you like football.'"

We stop talking, minutes pass, and Bill says, "But you know it's been fun with him. Maybe another could be fun too. Let's talk about it more when we get home."

I am looking at the stairway. Bill has been scraping the paint off since we got home from our trip eight weeks ago. Staring at the different layers of paint—blue, red, and brown—I think God has knocked Bill down flat. Bill's pinnacle job is gone. Actually, the three of us have lost something. I want a sibling for Bill J, Bill J wants a sister, and a second adoption is not possible without another salary.

Our Higher Power, I reflect, *wants us to go in a different direction. He wants us to travel to our next best stop.* I smile, thinking I have it all settled, when I recall Bill screaming one night as I was walking in from work: "*Why did you do this? Why did you do this?*"

"Hon, who are you yelling at?"

"God. *He* can take it!"

I smile, because that is exactly what I want to do. Standing by the stairway, I yell: "*Why did you do this? Why did you do this?*"

Two weeks later, I am again surveying how much paint has been scraped off the stairway. It is a measure of how Bill is feeling—more paint gone, he is feeling a little better. Suddenly, I hear a voice on the answering machine: "Joan Hoey, your appointment with the doctor is tomorrow at two-thirty. Please let the office know today if you cannot keep the appointment."

I walk away from the stairway into the kitchen, smiling that I had forgotten about the appointment. It was made before the trip to DC, which seems like years ago.

I am looking at the list of doctors in the building. I admonish myself for always forgetting where her office is, and then I see 406. Walking into the waiting room, I notice women of all ages. A photograph of a group of diverse women travels across my mind with the caption: "Women of Strength." Smiling, I muse, "How fitting for a gynecologist's office."

My doctor walks into the office. "Hi, Joan."

I look at her short auburn hair and her warm smile and feel relief. Once we're inside her office, she looks at my chart and says, "Joan, you need a total hysterectomy."

"I'm not surprised, given the fibroid discussions."

"You seem to be taking this well. Are you as okay as you look?" she asks.

"Well, yes and no," I respond. "I have my son, and as you know, adoption was my preference."

"Right, you've told me you never attempted to get pregnant and—"

"But the no is Bill's job has been eliminated, and I'm wondering about how I'm going to—"

"Pay for it? Let's not worry right now about that."

Driving home, I am dazed. Stopping at a red light, an epiphany happens. Maybe my Higher Power is letting me know that wanting a second child so Bill J can have a sibling is not the right reason for a second adoption. Yes, the operation is real, but symbolically, it means no more children.

———

However, several weeks later, the endless tape repeats: Is it selfish of us not to provide a sibling for our son? Would he be compromised in some way? Struggling, I begin to pray for another child while walking from my office to dinner at a Mexican restaurant. Passing The Neighborhood Music School, with thunder boomeranging in my brain, I feel a strong pull in the pit of my stomach as I pass The Foundry Book Store. Ignoring it, I continue to the Mexican restaurant. Savoring the refried beans in my mouth, reveling in the respite from the disturbing thoughts, I clean my plate. As I leave the restaurant and head back to my office, the bookstore comes into view, and the pull is back.

I shout, "All right!" and quickly look around, hoping no one heard me. I walk down the concrete stairs into the bookstore. The owner, a short, dark-haired man with glasses asks if he can help me. I almost burst out laughing, thinking, *If you only knew*. Instead, I answer, "No thank you." I feel his eyes on me as I stop and stare at each book. Turning the corner, the title *Maybe One: A Personal and Environmental Argument for Single Child Families* hits me.[8]

I pull up a stool and read. The author and his wife have a daughter, their only child. The questions that circled my mind are answered. After extensive research, the author discovered only children are not more compromised than any other child. He and his wife decided not to have another child. They did not feel guilty.

"Thank you, HP, from the bottom of my heart," I whisper. "And I'm sorry about the attitude."

My Higher Power knew I was struggling, and He pointed the right direction—another sibling was not needed. A nanosecond later, I recall Marge Turcott saying to Bill and me before we went to Peru: "The wee one wants a life this time where he knows he will be loved. And where his parents will have the time to love him."

I feel like a vending machine, if it could feel when the dollar has reached the bottom of the slot. A brother or sister would take time away from him. I chuckle and say to God, "I sure am dense. You let me know this awhile ago. Thanks for the repetition."

It is nine weeks later. I have had the operation. Our insurance carried over, and Bill has gotten a job at one-third of his former salary. I am happy to have my energy back.

We have just finished dinner, and I am telling Bill how much Bill J loves the new day care he recently moved to. Bill's head moves slightly down; his eyes look dull. He says, "That's good—there are more kids his own age."

It has been two years since his dream job has been eliminated, and he has gotten a position as an employee assistant at a psychotherapy practice. My heart sinks seeing his hurt. I decide for me and for him to let him talk about his current job.

"How's it going at the practice?" I ask.

"Okay."

"Really?"

"Oh, it is so boring. I like to be busy, and there is nothing to do," he admits. "It's so boring."

"Bill, you're a bright guy; of course you're bored. This job is an entry-level job. Leave it."

"Leave it?" His voice is hard and louder.

"Yes, leave it," I repeat.

"And what do you think would be my next move?"

"Graduate school—get your MSW. Look, an entry-level position is never going to be satisfying. You've worked at higher levels, and through your natural smarts, you've managed to rise through the ranks of several drug and alcohol facilities. Don't you see, your Higher Power wants you to move in a different direction."

I hear the chair scrape back as he gets up quickly. He's collecting the dishes. Rushing to hold him, he breaks away and says, "I can't go to school. I've got a family to support." I feel his eyes boring into mine.

"Bill, I have a profession. I have a full caseload. True, it's not the same as two salaries, but we can do it. We can rent our house and live in an apartment."

"*No way. We won't do that. No way!*"

I hear the banging of the garbage pails outside as Bill is releasing his frustration. "Please, God, help him. Help us."

The next morning I awake, knowing I will not mention graduate school again. I feel calm; I feel like an angel has visited me and has given me clarification. Pushing Bill to graduate school, if I could, would be shooting my marriage in the foot; resentment would be the result. Bill, through his Higher Power's guidance, will decide what is for his highest best.

———∽∽∽◦◦⇝◦⇜◦◦∽∽∽———

I am walking to the mailbox; the calm has remained. The spring air feels good against my cheeks, and the sweetness of flowers are in my nose. The flap of the mailbox creaks as I pull it down and gather the envelopes and advertisements. I notice the return address of the judicial department of the City of New Haven. I hurry into the house and phone Bill.

"Hi. There is a letter from the probation department. Do you want me to open it and read it to you?"

"Yes. I'm a hatcheck person for the event today."

The boring job ended, and he has been working as a waiter at a banquet facility.

"Smile your best smile, and you'll get tips. Okay, here goes: 'Dear Mr. Hoey, Thank you for your application. We are sorry to inform you—'"

"That's enough, got it, no go."

"I'm sorry, hon; the cut off age is thirty-five."

"Well, I'm young enough to be a hatcheck person."

"Yeah, and you have a terrific build."

Putting down the phone, although I feel bad for Bill's disappointment, I am more convinced our Higher Power is continuing to put obstacles in Bill's path, for he turned thirty-eight three days ago. Yes, I think: *you sure want him to travel in a different direction. You're responsible for the quick sand. Help me stay on dry land and hold onto your rope. Give me your grace to throw Bill the rope as each job is denied.*

The water feels cool on my bare feet as Bill J is spraying his trucks. I realize it has been several months since I read the letter to Bill. Bill J's voice breaks through my thought.

"Let's make a big hill so the trucks can smash into the lake," he says.

I feel the mud oozing between my toes. "Okay," I agree. My shins are in the mud, and I am thrilled. I look at Bill J's mud-splattered face and arms as he moves mounds of dry dirt to the edge of the pit that use to hold a huge outdoor pool.

"Mom, watch this." He sends a small gray truck down the hill to the lake, which is a mud hole that has to be continually filled with water. "Did you see that?" He's laughing, and I am laughing at his laughter. "It didn't even get close."

"Try a bigger one."

I see his grip on a miniature eighteen-wheeler. I am thankful for the cold water from the hose on this ninety-five-degree day. Our eyes are glued to the truck's journey when I hear Bill's voice. "It might just make it."

The truck is left, and Bill J yells, "Daddy, Daddy!"

Bill picks him up, the mud smearing against his uniform. He looks at me. "You look beautiful!" His eyes are twinkling.

I chuckle and say: "Another romantic compliment from Bill Hoey." We wash off, and I squirt Bill from head to toe.

Walking to the house, Bill J says: "I got Daddy more than you, and you lost because you're the wettest."

"Well, I think you're going to be the wettest, because in the tub you go."

Purposeful Destiny

As I watch Bill take off his waiter clothes, I notice his movements are slower than usual. When I catch a glimpse at his face, he looks not just the usual tired but as if something is on his mind—something weighing on him. I hear him and Bill J in the shower. Bill J is chattering, and I realize his father has granted him the joy of joining him under the water.

Everyone is cleaned up, and Bill's hair is glistening from the shower as the sun through the French doors bounces off it. While pouring iced tea, I say, "How did it go? Was it crazy busy?"

"No, it was dead."

"Dead?"

"There weren't any parties. I was cleaning grease traps—grease traps in the kitchen."

My stomach drops. I am about to say, "Oh my God, you don't have to do that—just come home," when I see he is going to say something.

"Joan, it was so hot—so hot you almost couldn't breathe. I've got to get out of there."

I am still thinking, *How about graduate school?* The words are ready to gush out of my mouth when he looks down.

As he slowly lifts his head up, he says: "I was thinking about Fordham. They have an MSW program."

I get out of my chair so quickly it almost hits the floor. We hug and hug. He shouts "Hoey Dance," and Bill J comes running in from the living room. Bill picks up our son with one arm, and the three of us, arms locked, jump around shouting, "Hoey Dance, Hoey Dance." It's a tradition Bill started to cheer me when it became obvious he was the preferred parent.

Driving to work, I am thanking my Higher Power for the grease traps. "You sure knew the circumstance that would open Bill's mind to graduate school. Thank You, thank You, thank You." Finishing the last thank you, Becky, a former client, visits my mind. I see her jet-black hair and her big, dark eyes and recall our early work. She is telling me she works at McDonald's. Becky is twenty-eight and is a college graduate. She says when asked if she likes her job: "It's a job."

"Why are you there? You have a degree."

"I don't know. I just don't know. My partner said I should see you."

Remembering her sad eyes, I envision her feet stuck in cement and being pulled down in the ocean.

"I would like you to make a list of one hundred things you like, but while making it, don't think of jobs." Her face is a freeze frame with lips forming an F-bomb and eyes big.

You know like: "I like coffee. I like the beach. I like the color pink."

"That's frigging stupid—oh, I'm sorry—I didn't mean—"

"No worries. Will you do the list?"

"I don't know."

The next week she is reading her list to me. I smile as I recall what she read. "I like to make lists, I like to argue. I like a fair deal."

"Have you ever thought of becoming a lawyer?"

"I don't know if I can keep coming here. I don't see the point."

"The point is you're bored at your job. You're very smart but don't think you are, and you are outside your comfort zone."

"You can say that—" She looks toward the door, staring at it, her feet are pointed in that direction when slowly she turns toward me and says, "You really think I'm smart, or are you just blowing smoke?"

"I don't blow smoke at clients. You're smart."

One year later, she has been admitted to a prestigious law school, she has been chosen for law review (an honor only 10 percent of students make), and today she practices law.

While parking my car, I am happy and relieved that like Becky, Bill and I have grabbed the rope God threw us. It is a beautiful September day, the air is crisp, and the leaves are entertaining us with a myriad of colors as Bill and I are driving to Fordham University. We are en route to an orientation for a master's in social work. It feels good to be on the same page. We see the quaint stone buildings and follow other people into a large auditorium. I look around and notice there are more women than men. A slightly overweight woman walks to the podium; she is wearing glasses and is somewhere between her late thirties and early forties. We are listening to her description of the various concentrations.

She signals for questions when a thin man asks: "How much does it cost?"

It feels like the audience has become dead still. She says the cost per credit, when the man asks: "Help me. How much is that a year?"

"Twenty-five thousand," the woman answers.

I feel Bill's body stiffen. We squeeze each other's hands and mouth the word *loans*. Walking out, I hear a curly haired woman saying to another woman: "Well, did you think it was going to be free?"

Once in the car, I say in a somber tone, "The main goal is to stay out of jail."

Bill looks at me, and we burst out laughing. His smile slides to a serious expression. "The most important bills to be paid are the big and small mortgages."

"Right. The others can be paid as we can—"

"Or, a couple of dollars on a regular basis."

"Hon, I think we should sell one of the cars to cut down on insurance and upkeep."

Silence interrupts the rapid exchanges, and Bill says, "Yeah."

While feeling a ray of sun on my face coming through the windshield, I recall Bill J's first day on the roller skates his grandmother gave him. Clump, clump goes the skates on the grass before we reach the street. His fingers are like a vice around my hand. The vice gets tighter on the pavement, when suddenly he slips and misses the ground by several feet. He wriggles and regains his balance, looks up at me, and says: "Mom, that was a false alarm slide."

"It sure was," I agree.

We are both chuckling with relief.

Bill and I, I muse, are going through a false alarm slide. Two weeks later, he is accepted into the program. He waits tables at the banquet hall, sometimes twenty hours a day, and I continue to see clients. We are down to one car.

I am gathering my appointment book and keys to the office and take one last look in the mirror before walking out to the car. "Bill, I'll drive you to Woodwinds."

"No, you'll be late."

"No, I won't."

Before I can insist again, I see he is out in the street, in front of our house, in his waiter uniform. I see his thumb out. *Oh my God, he's hitchhiking.* I yell out to him, "Bill, wait." He turns his head, smiles the most mischievous smile, and is swept away by an

Purposeful Destiny

unknown driver. My heart is both heavy and light; the warmth of a tear slides down my cheek, and a laugh is forming in my throat. Bounding into my mind like an express train is a single thought: *I love him.*

Bill was not the only one hopping a ride. Bill J's ride to school is a stroller. I am anticipating a fuss from the big kindergartner, but he smiles when I say, "Let's see if we can beat the bus." Running, holding tightly on to the stroller, I screech to a halt before the main entrance. I watch the kindergartener join his friends. And, yes, we beat the bus.

Several days later, I am riding in a taxi to work, because a cab ride is cheaper than the upkeep of a second car. The driver, who was a high school athlete, is chattering pleasantries. I answer, but playing across my mind is that Bill J is going to do setup with his father at Woodwinds. I feel the angst of any mother hoping this was the right decision.

I hear the voice of Jan, our neighbor who Bill J stays with on Saturdays. "He's getting mouthy. I think he misses Saturdays with his father."

The two nights of setup at Woodwinds are compensation for the Saturdays Bill J and his dad used to spend together before Bill started graduate school.

"You can drop me here," I say to the taxi driver. The "here" is several blocks from my office.

"Tomorrow?" asks the cab driver.

"Yes," I respond. I am relieved Bill will be dropping the car off later, and he and Bill J will ride back to the banquet hall with a coworker.

I glance at the clock behind the office couch, knowing I cannot be late picking up Bill and Bill J. Jeb and Carol are the last clients of the day. They are a few minutes late. I hear the front door buzzer and walk up the stairs to greet them. Jeb has wavy blond hair and is thirty-three. Carol is extremely attractive with green eyes and jet-black hair. She is also thirty-three. They sit on the couch but almost at opposite ends. Carol bursts into tears, and Jeb rolls his eyes.

"He doesn't appreciate all I do," Carol cries. "He has a nine-to-five schedule as a banker, and I have a 24/7 schedule since the baby was born. He comes home and sits on the couch."

"Not true," Jeb says. "I come in, and you're on your cell talking to Pat."

"Who's Pat?" I ask.

"She's my best friend, and she listens to me. I tell her everything."

I ask her: "How do you like being married to Pat?"

She glares at me.

"Look, you can make a voodoo doll of me when you get home and stick pins in it," I say.

"No, I wouldn't do that," she notes.

"The two of you are the co-presidents of your family. If you were the co-presidents of a manufacturing company, you wouldn't call a worker off the assembly line and tell him intimate details of the business and leave your partner out of the loop. That would be making the assembly line worker a co-president without the official title."

They both defrost a little as they listen.

"Jeb, you need to get off the couch and have a business meeting with your wife," I suggest. The session ends with the agreement that they will come in next time with preliminary explicit agreements of how their "company" will work.

Purposeful Destiny

I quickly turn off the office lights, lock the office door, and get into the car Bill dropped off. I am hoping a cop does not stop me. I am going seventy miles an hour in a fifty-five-mile-an-hour zone. I have to make it to the truck stop before Bill and Bill J get there. I see eighteen-wheelers as I find a parking spot. I am looking around when I see the top of my husband's head. The night lights bounce off his black-brown hair. He is pushing a bundle in a stroller up the hill closest to the truck stop. Bill J bursts out of the bundle. His face is flushed with excitement. I look in Bill's eyes. I see tiredness. He breaks into a smile when he sees me seeing him.

"The little guy is dying to tell you something that—"

Bill J breaks in. "Mom, I know how to fold napkins. Right, Dad?"

"Right."

"Mom, I helped Daddy put down the wooden floor!"

"Wow! You're smart and strong."

"Can I touch the trucks *now*?" Bill J asks.

"Sure," I say, "but don't you want to see the real truck drivers inside?"

He touches a huge Weiner semitruck and looks like he's hearing angels singing. Then, without a look toward us, he runs into the truck stop. We yell, but he keeps moving. My heart stops and beats again when no cars or trucks hit him. Relieved, we walk into the eatery, find seats, and order dinner.

A bearded man is sitting next to Bill J. He says, "Hey, little fella, I saw you touching my truck." Frowns are forming on his face.

Bill squeezes Bill J's hand, and our son is dumbstruck.

His voice grows louder. "I don't like people touching my truck."

Bill has his mouth open, ready to spout, when the trucker breaks into loud guffaws. We see his missing teeth. "Hey, I'm a softie." He sees our annoyed faces. "Sorry, I was just messing wit you." He sticks out his hand. "My name's Zeg."

Before taking his hand, Bill says, "No more messing, Zeg," and then shakes his hand.

After several volleys, Bill J pipes up. "My truck is cleaner than yours."

Zeg laughs so hard he is slapping the counter with his hand. "Now *that's* messing." Thirty minutes later, Bill J is sitting behind the steering wheel of Zeg's Weiner semitruck. We all say good night, with smiles all around. Driving home, I notice the smudge and dirt on Bill's uniform, and I chuckle. Bill looks at me, knowing I am replaying the truck stop scene.

"Quite the night ... not too shabby for Bill J sitting behind the wheel of the Weiner truck," Bill says.

"Yeah," I respond. "It looked like he was catapulted to heaven."

Two days later, I still feel energized by the night at the truck stop. I am thankful that I do, because my first client is a woman who has miscarried her first child. Sarah has brown hair, is a lawyer, and is twenty-nine. I put the box of tissues next to her, because the tears and sobs are continuous.

"I wanted this baby so, so much ... Dan and I ... Dan and I—"

She is racked with sobs, and I ask if I can hug her. She looks shocked. I take it as a definite no.

"We picked out the colors for the nursery ... pink and white. Her name is—I mean, was going to be Jennifer." She looks up at the low ceiling of the office and angles her eyes toward me. "So, what words of wisdom do you have for me?"

Purposeful Destiny

"Continue mourning. You can decide not to climb uphill, but keep the feet moving."

"What the f—— does that mean?" she snaps at me.

"It means continue mourning but don't give up. Six weeks, six months, a year from now—"

"Oh, you think I'll be over this? *I'll never be over this!*"

"Your right; you probably won't. But at some point, it may be helpful to peruse Sylvia Browne's book *Conversations with the Other Side*."[9]

She leaves. Another appointment is not made.

Several months later while I am billing insurance companies, the office phone rings. I pick it up; there is no greeting. "Why didn't you *tell* me the soul of a baby can decide it's not the right time to be born but can be born at another time?"

"Hi, Sarah. To answer your question, I didn't think you could hear it at that time. I just kept my feet moving."

She laughs. "So did I, but that's not the only thing I kept moving. I'm pregnant."

"Oh, I'm so happy for you," I say.

"Joan, do you believe in a … a … *Universe* … an … *Energy*?"

"Higher than myself? Absolutely! Who do you think sent you to me?"

"Can I make an appointment?" Sarah asks.

"Sure, but why?"

"I want to pick your brain about the Universe thing."

Six months later, Sarah and Dan will become the parents of a seven-pound girl.

Driving home, I am happy for Sarah and Dan. I am smiling about Sarah's gleefulness when I feel my throat tighten. *"Father's Day—this Sunday. Oh no, how am I going to do it?* I think to myself.

Wham—call Marie and ask to borrow money, says a tiny voice inside my mind's eye. Walking up the driveway, I am glad Bill's car is not in the driveway. I call the Essex Steam Train, an old, authentic steam train. I will need $160 for an elegant Father's Day lunch in their dining car. I punch in Marie's number.

I hear her voice with a smile in it. "Hi, Sister," she says.

"Hi, Marie. Sister, can you lend me $160? I'll pay you back. It might be in increments. I want Bill to have a great Father's Day."

"Sure, Joanie, I could lend you more."

"No, $160 will do it."

"You sure?"

"Yup, you're a doll," I tell her. "I love you."

Bill J looks at me with excitement in his eyes. I explain we are going to take Daddy for a ride on a real steam train.

"We'll see the engine, right?" he asks.

"Right."

"We're going to sit right next to it!"

"I don't know about right next to it but up front in the open car," I assure him.

"Tomorrow?" He is fidgeting.

"No, three days from now. Don't tell Daddy—it's a surprise." I am sorry he overheard my conversation with Marie. I decide to bribe him.

Father's Day arrives, and Bill is reading the handwritten message of the card out loud, smiling with his eyebrows arched: "Today may be bumpy?" He looks at Bill J, who bursts out laughing. Next, he looks at me holding a scarf in my hand. "Oh no—what's that for?" he asks.

"Bend down. You'll know soon." I tie the scarf around his head. "Can you see?"

"No."

"Are you sure?"

Purposeful Destiny

"Yes. Where are we going?"

"To the car," I tell him. Bill J and I lead him to the car parked in the driveway. Giggles are escaping like bubbles as we say, "Get in the backseat." I give Bill J a thumbs-up as we drive. We see the sign for the Essex Steam Train, and I put a finger up to my lips to quiet Bill J. We pull in, and I say to Bill, "You can take off the blindfold."

Bill looks at us, his eyes twinkling. We walk into the dining car. A maître d' ushers us to a table. An elegant card seems to glare: "Hoey 3." Bill smiles, head down, his face filled with emotion. He slowly moves his head up and says, "How did you pull this off?"

"Magic," I tell him.

"Not too shabby."

Between courses, we take Bill J to the front car by the engine; black flakes are in our hair. The steam climbs up the sky, and the whistle blows loudly. The train jerks to a stop at Deep River, and we board a ferry and ride up the Connecticut River.

The Father's Day celebration has given me the strength to confront the mailbox and the threats of "pay now or else." On one of the envelopes, I see the words *Esser & Esser* and in smaller letters *attorneys of law*. The muscles on the back of my neck are tightening. I rip open the envelope and spot the word *lien*.

A bee is buzzing inside my head as I calculate the week's income from my practice. Walking back to the house, the question blaring in my mind is: *Do I tell Bill tonight?* A loud *no* is the response, followed by: *He's working twenty hours today.* I realize as I am playing battleship with Bill J that my mind has been switching stations from terror to our smiles inside the Essex Steam Train. Then, a huge flash goes off in my mind.

Turning to Bill J, I say, "Let's get dressed up funny for when Daddy comes home."

"Okay. Do we have to stop playing?"

"No, I mean way later tonight."

The joker's hat on my head keeps slipping down. As I push it up with my index finger, I glance over at junior. He is dressed as Popeye, and his small hand is holding up the other end of the sign whose red letters announce: "It's No Joke Working Twenty Hours A Day."

I whisper, "I hear him."

Bill walks in; he is wearing his leather bomber jacket. He looks in the library and then the dining room, breaking into a laugh. "Look at the two of you. My God, where did you get that hat?" He takes it off my head and puts it on. He picks up Popeye. As he lifts him, he says he is not sure his muscles are strong enough. The night goes on, and I put Bill J to bed.

Walking down the stairs, I notice Bill still has his bomber jacket on. His eyes look mischievous. They direct me to the jacket's zipper. He is slowly moving the zipper down. I see the corner of a plastic container, and when he notices that I do, he opens the jacket. "Chicken bolognaise, shrimp, veal cordon blue—all for you and yours, madam."

I am laughing and feel relief surge through me. I know the grocery money saved will not pay the lien, but I feel a surge of relief anyway. "How did you get all that to fit in your jacket? And how did you keep it from not slipping out?"

"Wait."

I watch his hand move close to his armpit, and slowly, the top of a coffee can appears. "You're amazing."

"You keep saying that—"

"I'll stop if it makes you feel better!"

"Oh, um … no."

Purposeful Destiny

Penny is sitting on the office couch. She is fifty-five and attractive. She is grieving her mother's recent death. "I just don't get it," she says to me. "I thought by now I'd be further along." She is reaching for the tissues and blowing her nose.

"According to whom?" I ask her. "If there is only *one* schedule, I have never heard of it. You're making progress. Look, I want you to think of some escape hatches."

Her eyes are question marks. "My wish for you is to create a time twice a day when you decide not to grieve."

"You think I'm being miserable on purpose? My God!" she gasps.

"No, I think you need to take breaks. Deliberate breaks like listening to music that really moves you, rearranging your closet, because you told me once you would love to rearrange people's closets for a living."

She smiles in recognition, which is quickly wiped away by a frown. "I would feel guilty doing that—you know, selfish."

"Penny, you've told me awhile ago you believe in heaven. Your mother is there; she knows you love her."

She turns her head toward a decorative screen and says, "So you're saying it's okay not to think of mom 24/7? I won't be a bad daughter, and my mother will love me?"

"Exactly, and I would pick specific times for the breaks."

Looking triumphant, she says, "How do you know she won't be disappointed?"

"Let's just say it's a gut feeling. But it might become more real if you hear it echoed by Dr. Michael Newton in *Destiny of the Soul* and by James Van Praagh in *Talking to Heaven*."

In my break before the next client, a thousand mosquitoes are buzzing inside my body. A nightmare is playing in my mind: I am telling the next client to shut up. I am burning out. I feel I am losing it. I tell Rosemary, the next client, I do not feel well and am going home. I cancel the rest of the day's clients. My hand is trembling as I push the unlock button for the car. I call Bill; tears are racing down my cheeks. I hear his voice, and sobs burst out. "I almost said 'shut up' to a client. I am burning out."

"You've been seeing twenty or twenty-one clients in three days. You need rest. Don't worry, don't worry. Cancel the rest of your clients."

Driving home, I feel terror. Questions form: What if I cannot continue my practice? What if I do not like my clients anymore? I start praying, and the knowingness that I must rest helps me.

Five days later, I am reminiscing about the at-home vacation. Bill had arranged playdates for Bill J and asked neighbors to help me. It is Sunday, and the sunshine is streaming through the open windows. I look at Bill; he is not wearing his uniform. He takes my hand, smiles widely, and says, "I swapped shifts. We're going swimming—a vacation day."

We park our car on a dirt patch. The three of us and Tyler, our golden retriever, scramble out. I scan the lake for other dogs and see Labradors, spaniels, and beautiful mutts. Voices and laughter permeate the air. It boosts the joy, and I am feeling a notch higher. Bill J tugs at my T-shirt: "Mom, all the people stopped."

Bill looks at him and says, "Hey, why don't you get on my shoulders. You can tell us what's going on."

"There's a big kid," Bill J reports. "Ah … he's stopping people."

"He's probably double-checking if we live in the town."

We inch closer. There is a skinny teenager sitting behind a table. Bill pulls out a library card borrowed from a resident. There are pimples on the teenager's face. He does not look like this is "just a summer job."

Purposeful Destiny

"The admission for the three of you is twelve dollars," he says.

"What?" Bill growls. "Look, we rushed out. Could I bring you the money later?"

I know we do not have the money, but then I realize Bill is thinking about the penny jar.

"No, sir. I'm afraid you can't gain entrance unless you pay now." His voice is a good cop imitation.

Red is inching up Bill's throat. He turns to me, face flushed. I grab his hand and whisper, "Let's sneak in past the fence."

"Right."

We pass people, pass the wooden fence, drop our blanket, and run straight into the water. "Yes! Yes! Yes!" we shout as the cold water envelops us.

The next day I smile at our rebellion and our swimming the last hour in the beach proper. Later that night, I tell Bill, "I'm so relieved I am my usual self with clients."

Bill is drinking coffee and gathering notes for a paper due Monday. "I knew all you needed was a break and a very special swim."

"Let's hear it for pimple-faced cops!" A chuckle is in my throat.

Bill holds up the key to Bev and Tom Kidder's office, fellow social workers who have lent Bill their New Haven office. Several hours later, the phone rings. I pick it up, thinking Bill's giving me a heads-up for dinner. He sounds too excited for a usual supper call. "Joan, I needed a quote, so I pulled the *Social Work Encyclopedia* down from the shelf—and you won't believe what I saw—"

"William Hoey gets an A in a boring class?"

"You're close."

"Oh, sure."

His voice, half an octave lower, continues: "It was a heading. I was copying a reference when on the opposite page I saw: *Jane Hoey*."[10]

"What? Are you—"

"Jane Hoey, it turns out, was a prominent social worker. Joan, she even worked at the United Nations."

"Oh, my God, Bill."

"Yeah. Oh my God."

It is 2013, and the three of us are sitting in Bryant Park Grill. We have ordered dinner, before seeing a Broadway show. Bill J (now twenty-two) is seated next to Bill. I notice the glint in his eye as he begins to fold the napkin.

He looks at Bill and says, "Remember this?"

They race to finish a fancy folding. Bill graduated from Fordham in 1997. He has held a series of high-level positions. But I believe his current position as vice president of mission services at a busy hospital has been his favorite. Watching them, I think of a Ray Bradbury quote: "Living a life of risk is like jumping off a cliff and building your wings on the way down."[11] And I muse by noticing God's reassurances along the way and the knowingness that He pushed us off in the first place. I wondered if this happened to Bill J when he asked for a sister, so long ago, and noticed HP's guidance. After a playdate with Nick, who had a younger sister, Bill J told us, "I don't want a sister, and I'm glad I don't have one."

The bridge across forever exists. Recognizing it will bring you joy, love, and direction.

Wonder Bread: A Father's Second Chance from Heaven

Purposeful Destiny

It is 1980, nine years before Bill and I are married, and I am walking through the revolving door of a Long Island hospital. I see anxious and sad faces in the lobby. I make my way to the elevator and push the button for the second floor. I hear the ding of the elevator, and as I step out, the smell of disinfectants, perspiration, and body odor hit me. As I move along, out of the corner of my eye I see an elderly woman scrunched up who is moaning.

I recall my brother's telephone call: "Joanie, Dad's been transferred to Long Island."

A picture of a crushed car, one that looks like it's been twisted and flattened by the machine at a scrap metal yard, floats across my mind. It's the car Dad was thrown thirty-five feet through the windshield, resulting in him being in a Syracuse hospital for a year. Now, a year later, walking down the hall of this Long Island hospital, the green walls make me want to puke; my stomach is queasy. I arrive at Dad's room. He does not see me. I stifle a scream as I see his hair has not been washed, and his toenails look like snakes. He opens his eyes and sees me walking toward him. He cannot talk; he is on a ventilator. Holding his cold hand, I realize I do not love him. I feel the sadness I would feel for an acquaintance. Guilt engulfs me from head to toe. As his fingers interlock with mine, a scene tumbles through my mind.

My sister Marie, my brother Johnny, and I are doing the after-dinner dishes. Marie is a teenager; my brother and I are younger than ten years old. Marie is washing, Johnny is drying, and I am putting away. I place the small pots into bigger pots so they are like a family. Before dinner the next night, Dad walks in from work, and he is unloosening his tie. His face grows dark. He says pointing to the kitchen table, "Who did this?"

I am scared. I don't know what he means.

Again, he says: "Who did this?"

I now see the drawer in the table has been carved. It is a new kitchen table.

Marie says, "I didn't do it."

Johnny says, "I didn't do it."

I say the same thing, but I start to cry.

Dad says, "Well if you didn't do it, then why are you crying?"

"I don't know," I say, and I cry harder. His voice ridged, he tells me to go into the dining room. He stands in front of a picture of the Virgin Mary. Mary is wearing a long dress, and there are stars around her head. He says, "If you didn't do it, say it in front of the Virgin Mary."

"I didn't do it." My heart is pounding, and tears are spilling down my cheeks. He smacks me.

Immediately, Johnny says, "I did it."

Dad yells, "Anne, pack Johnny's clothes. He's going to Boys Town." He shows Johnny a picture of the place and says, "You'll have to scrub concrete floors."

I hear the suitcase clanging down the stairs. He tells Johnny to put his coat on. Johnny is crying. Dad is opening the front door.

I scream, "Please don't make Johnny go."

The suitcase is put down, and Johnny gets to live with us still.

A tugging at my sleeve brings me back. I see the chalkboard Dad is holding up. I am startled. He has written: "Get me out of here."

I respond, "John, if I unplug you, you won't make it past the lobby. Think about if this is really what you want."

He does not repeat the request. Two months later, he passed away on Valentine's Day 1980.

Twelve years later, 1992, a few days after Valentine's Day, I am washing the dishes. The warm water feels soothing on my hands. Raffi is singing "Down by the Bay."[12] I am singing along, and every now and then Little Bill looks at me with mischief in his eyes. I follow the hands of my two-year-old and see he is taking the pots out of the cabinet. I hear the clang as he bangs them together.

I say, "What fun, eh?"

My mind shifts to the day I prayed to my father to lift the terror I was not Little Bill's authentic mother. The fear disappeared, and I chuckled, thinking maybe heaven has changed my father. Then rushing as if it was on fire, I see Carl's face, a client I'd worked with in the past.

Pow—it hits me. God sent Carl so I could see how Dad suffered. Carl was a portal. Talking to God in my mind's eye, I say, "*Thank you for Carl. It only took me twelve years to recognize what You wanted me to know—talk about being dense!*"

Focusing more on Carl, I see his shoes. They are highly polished. Dad's shoes always shined. Not one of Carl's hairs is out of place; his fingernails are trimmed and manicured. He looks like he could conquer the world, and that was my father's persona. I see Carl's tears, spilling down his cheeks, releasing his fears and hurts. I realize my father kept the frightened little boy of himself behind a wall. I remember Carl's response of "absolutely" to the question: "So, maybe all this time you thought saying your true feelings would cause Valerie (his former wife) to get angry?"

"I thought my agreement with whatever she wanted would make her happy," he'd said.

"She didn't see this as generosity?"

"No."

———〜〜·ᄋ·ᄋ·〜〜———

It is a summer Sunday. I am eight years old, and we are going to Alley Pond State Park. The family goes every Sunday.

Mom says, "It's Grandma's summer home."

All the food is packed, and everyone is psyched. Dad moves slowly to the coffee pot; he walks across the kitchen and takes out a cup. He pours the coffee into the cup and drinks it slowly.

Mom says, "Johnny, we're late. Don't you want to go?"

"Yes, I'm coming." He takes out his cigarettes, Camels, slowly brings his head down, and strikes a match.

I feel like I am going to burst. I am saying to myself: "Let's go! Let's go!"

He doesn't move. He stands there and inhales his cigarette. "Johnny, if you don't want to go, just say so," Mom says.

"I want to go."

I am relieved and happy.

Dad's behavior that day mirrors Carl before Carl's therapy ended. Dad was afraid to say his true feelings. He was afraid of conflict and was terrified of emotion. But unlike Carl and many other clients I have treated, my father was horrifically abused by his alcoholic immigrant father who tied him in the basement and beat him until he soiled his pants.

Mauro, my grandfather, would not let him change his pants until his brothers were called downstairs to see his tear-strewn face and smell the odor of soiled pants. I believe Dad made a decision to tuck this boy behind a wall, so he would never cave again. On the other side of the wall is Superman, who can accomplish all external goals. His children, wife, in-laws, and coworkers only saw Superman John.

John was further abused when his father would not allow him to go to high school, especially after having been skipped two grades in elementary school. I recall Dad telling the story:

My father refused to let me go to high school. My godfather, Vito, went to speak to him, and I stayed in the bathroom hearing Vito's voice.

"Mauro, Johnny is so smart, just like you," he said. "But in America he needs an education. My God, who else of your children have been skipped two grades? Jesus, he could go to college."

"Vito, mind your own goddamn business," my father said. "What's school going to do? Is it going to toughen him up? Is it going to make a man out of him? He's a sissy boy. He helps his mother with the wash. C'mon."

"Look, there's plenty of time for him to become a man. He's only thirteen. Look, I'm serious. I'll pay for his college if you let him go to high school."

"Get out, Vito. Get out. You're sticking your nose up my ass. It's not your business."

I wish I hadn't been skipped two grades. I would have had two more years of school.

Fast-forward twenty years. Dad drives a Wonder Bread truck. His uniform is a dark twill jacket and pants. The jacket looks fashionable, ending fitted at the waist. Whoever does well in school gets to go on the truck like the time Dad and Mom went to open school night for my sister Marie.

Before Marie started school, he told her, "You must keep your eyes on the teacher all the time."

After the meeting, Dad walks into the house bursting with pride. He says to Marie, "Mrs. Frolick said, 'Oh, Marie's parents. Well, every day I feel those dark eyes of hers right here.'" Dad is making two spots on his forehead. "'And two right here.'" Dad's is marking two places on the back of his head. "'Would you please tell her she doesn't have to look at me every minute?'" Dad is laughing. His eyes are alive. He looks actually present in the moment. Marie gets to go on the truck. By the time I was old enough to go, Dad was working for the Prudential Insurance Company.

My father became more remote as time passed—less talk and more work. I believe he got worn down, angry. Disappointed neither his wife nor children could guess his preferences or comfort—the terrified boy hiding behind the Superman persona. I recall a New Year's Day.

I am a sophomore in college, Johnny is home from The New England School of Music, Marie and her husband are expecting their first child. We are all seated around the dining room table of our Babylon, New York, home. The dining room is beautiful. The lower halves of the walls are wainscoted. A deft blue-and-white wallpaper covers the rest of the walls. The furniture is new. A big hutch houses blue-and-white dishes. There is turkey, mashed potatoes, different bowls of vegetables, two types of olives, and assorted breads.

Dad says, "I told Pat the most important thing is to close and make a sale. He's just not getting it."

We all groan and say, "We've heard this story before."

His big blue eyes look down, his handsome face pensive. Seconds pass, he slowly lifts his head and says, "He's a nice man, but I'm trying to teach him to close."

Everyone nods as if the story is new. His words have no impact; I am behind my wall.

Purposeful Destiny

It is 1994, twenty years after the New Year's Day dinner. The phone rings, and I hear my brother's voice on the answering machine and pick up. "Hi, Johnny. How are you?"

"Good. I was just looking at some pictures Mom gave me, and I got to thinking about Dad."

"Wow, you must have mental telepathy," I tell him. "I've been thinking about him a lot today—how terrified I was around him. To hug him was to walk away feeling creepy. You know, his muscles were tight, he pulled away quickly, no tussle of the hair, no words of endearment. Oh, I bet your glad you called. I've had verbal diarrhea. Sorry."

"Well, I was going to ask you if you felt—like there was fresh air in the house when he wasn't home, because that's how I felt. I'm thinking more about my growing-up days. But what you just said kind of answered a lot. He was a workaholic, right? And he seemed to accomplish whatever he wanted, right?"

"Oh, yeah, you got that right. Remember when Mom said she'd like a kitchen window, and we walked down after shopping on Jamaica Avenue and saw a big hole in the side of the house?"

"Oh, the kitchen window. Geez, I forgot about that," he says. "And Uncle Joe told us when he found out about the window that Dad almost became an assemblyman until—" We are both laughing. "Until they ... until somebody told them he was nineteen." We're sputtering laughing. I'm slapping my thigh. "But he did work a lot."

"Yeah, a lot," I agree.

After hanging up the phone, I think for the first time, the very first time, that Dad was courageous. I chuckle at the incongruity of past thoughts and this new one. Dad was incredibly fearful, but he kept on keeping on. Again, if courage were a person, it would pray for fear, because fear is the engine that moves us to our next best stop. Sure, Dad did not get to his very best stop, but the fear in his belly kept him from stopping altogether. It was after this epiphany and the remembrance of asking Dad to eliminate the awful fear I was not Little Bill's authentic mother that I felt my relationship with my father was changing. The window cleaners were showing up and removing the dust and grime of the past inside me.

Two days later, Bill, Little Bill, and I bring our pillows and blankets into the living room. We take a nap. I dream about my father. He was hugging me lovingly. His whole body was relaxed—no more taut muscles, no more creepy feelings—hugging was no longer painful for him. I was hugging him back. It was the first full hug I ever got from him. He was showing me how to make dresses out of strawberries. We were laughing. Waking up, I feel we had played for the first time. I sense my father's soul existed.

Feeling this way, Carl's face crosses my mind as he said during one of our sessions: "Boy, you're really out there." I had spotlighted Dr. Michael Newton's book *Destiny of the Soul* where he describes client experiences while under regressive hypnotherapy. They repeatedly report about a library in heaven that allows them to view their past lives.[13] Sylvia Browne mentions the same opportunity for us and departed souls where not only past life events are recorded but also the feelings of those with whom we have interacted.[14]

I recall a man in a bereavement group I facilitated whose son, Joey, passed from a drug overdose. I remember him telling the members: "Yeah, of all people I dreamt about, I couldn't believe it was this asshole friend of my son, Martin, who obviously used drugs. Well, don't you know, a couple of days later this shit-for-brains guy is at my door. I didn't want to open the door for that scumbag, but I did. Martin tells me: 'I dreamt about Joey, and Joey kept telling me to tell you it was not your fault he died. He wanted me to tell you he was drug free and happy.'"

"If anybody told me I would be hugging Martin and we would be crying together, I would have told him he belonged in the nuthouse."

Joey experienced his father's feelings at the hall of records. I suggested to this father and the rest of the group that God does not want us to feel guilty. But I also imagined Dad at the hall of records viewing his past life, understanding the impact of frightening us into obedience, and being horrified and sorry.

It was shortly after the group that I began to notice Wonder Bread trucks. I would see them on I-95 and not attach any meaning to them, until the day after the three of us went to a hockey game. Pulling into our driveway after the game, Bill carrying Little Bill inside, he whispers, "I hope he doesn't wake up before I put him down." Walking down the stairs with his fingers crossed and no cries from our son's room, Bill takes my hand, and we sit on our couch. I sense something is bothering him.

"You look uneasy," I say as I squeeze his hand.

He says, "I found a lump on my body. I made an appointment with Wayne."

Terror engulfs me; both his parents died from cancer. Trying to be reassuring, I say, "It's probably just a cyst, and as you know, a cyst is mainly water."

"I hope so."

The next day I am sobbing while driving to work. A neon sign keeps flashing in my mind: "Bill's Got Cancer—Bill's Got Cancer." I feel tears dribbling down my neck. My collar feels squishy. A deep moan is making its way up my throat when a Wonder Bread truck pulls in front of me—literally, in front of my car. The Trumbull Street exit in New Haven is a narrow one.

The truck exits the highway and stays in front of me right past my office. I say, "Oh, Dad, is that you?"

Later that night Bill is all smiles. He tells me: "It's just a cyst. Wayne says I'm cancer-free."

I start jumping around the kitchen; Bill is laughing and joins me. Then, almost as an afterthought, he says, "By the way, on the way to Wayne's office I saw a Wonder Bread truck!"

I feel Dad's soul cares about me.

I wonder if he'll always be there for me? Driving home from the office several months later after seeing too many clients, I feel cranky. I do not want to bite Bill's head off when I get home. I test Dad and say, "Dad, I need your help."

Immediately—immediately—I see a Wonder Bread truck. It astonishes me. I feel jumbled; this is so unusual. Before Dad died, he had not attended my college graduation. He told me he had to work. Now, he was tuned in to me.

Later that night, I am standing in our library, looking at a picture of Mom and Dad and smiling to myself that I had not turned into a beast when I got home. I think, *They look smashing.* I am admiring their good looks. Mom's gown is elegant—no bows, no frills, the less-is-more concept. They are in a dance pose, arms out, hands entwined. Dad's tuxedo curves at the waist, accentuating his slim physic. I reach for the picture ready to kiss Mom as usual when I realize my arm has stopped midway. I bring the photo closer and kiss Dad for the first time.

The visits continue, and I smile, thinking about a conversation with my friend Terry. "Joan, you're probably passing a Wonder Bread truck whose route passes Trumbull Street." Her lawyer face frozen into "and that's that."

"Yeah, well my office hours vary, and they have pulled in front of my car on other side streets."

"Whatever."

"Whatever."

I decide not to tell Terry a bereavement anecdote to back up Dad's visits. Mary, a petite, ninety-pound woman in her forties tells the group: "My father, Walt, God I miss him. I miss watching movies with him; we both loved movies. I've heard stories in here about relationships continuing with our lost ones, but frankly, I didn't believe them until this past vacation. As you all know, my family and I went to the beach. I decided to take, you know, some alone time. I was walking to the ocean when I spotted a director's chair half buried in the sand. I walked right up to it and across the back was written 'Walt's Chair.'"

Mary beaks into a big smile. The group applauds enthusiastically.

Flipping the pages of my calendar, it is hard to believe it is 1995. The group ended a year ago, and Wonder Bread trucks still show up in times of need. I think back to the time I was burning out from a large caseload. Bill had arranged a week home for me and a vacation swimming day. The next day, before seeing my first client, I was nervous. I wondered if I was ready when I spotted a Wonder Bread truck slightly ahead of me. I felt I had been given an antibiotic for a life-threatening infection.

My relationship with Dad has grown stronger. The hungry feeling for positive attention from him is gone. I am his loved adult daughter.

I feel good as I anticipate Bill and Bill J's picking me up at the office. As I put papers away, I roll the name change from Little Bill to Bill J in my mouth to avoid slipping back to the former. The request made several months ago: "Mom, don't call me Little Bill. It's a baby name."

"Okay. What do you want your name to be?"

He looks down and then up and says: "Bill."

"How about JR for junior?"

His eyes bright, he says: "Bill J."

Delight is zooming inside me as I recall the conversation. The front door buzzer ends the reverie. I run up the stairs as Bill and Bill J are coming down. Bill is holding a picnic basket and a blanket. Smiles in his eyes, he says: "I thought we'd have a winter picnic."

We lay the blanket on the floor, away from the "living room" section. Bill J is looking to see where his latest Pokémon drawing is hanging. While passing the rolls and cold cuts, Bill says, "Bill J, tell Mommy what we saw today."

Bill J says, "We saw a Wonder Bread truck, and it's changed. It didn't have Hostess on it anymore. It just had Wonder Bread written all over it."

My husband says, "Yup, that's right."

My heart drops. "Oh no, this can't be the end of my relationship with Dad. That would be agony." *Maybe Dad is assuring me the change between us has been real and will always continue?* I thought to myself.

That night I dream of Dad. He says to me: "Look, no more pressure. The pressure is off me."

When I awake, I am happy for him. I tell him, "Dad, you deserve it. No more fright for you. That little boy of yours has scaled his wall. Good for you." But a nagging feeling persists. *Was that* really *Dad?* I wonder. He looked different—his hair was darker, his nose longer. Terror ensues.

The next day I drive to the office much earlier. The previous thoughts are still in my mind. "Please, Dad," I say, "please don't end this."

A Wonder Bread truck like my husband and son described moves from another lane in front of me and remains with me until

I get to my office. My heart leaps. "Oh, Dad, thank you, thank you, thank you."

It's 1998, and I am doing a second television show for CPT (Connecticut Public Television) on bereavement. As I wait for cars to pass before pulling into the studio, I am feeling nervous—very nervous. I say in my mind's eye, *"Dad, I wish you were here."*

I get as far as "wish," and a Wonder Bread truck passes by me. I am no more amazed than I was the day of my father-in-laws's funeral when Bill relayed a Wonder Bread truck passed him while en route to the cemetery.

Are these sightings still happening today? Yes. Our son reports he has seen a Wonder Bread truck before a "midcrit." He is an architect student, and midcrits are when the students' work is evaluated. My husband noticed one the first day he started his job at a hospital in southern Connecticut. I saw one yesterday, March 11, 2012, before a visit to Aunt Mae's (now ninety-one) who is deaf and blind in one eye. I had been anxious for the visit to go well.

Remember, our Higher Power will put obstacles in our way so that we will move in a different direction. He used the obstacle of fear that I was not my infant son's mother. It caused me to pray for my father's help. My Higher Power knew my feelings were not aligned regarding my father. He also knew Dad was now ready to have a full relationship with me. He wanted me to know relationships can continue after death.

The Lake:
A Loving Mother Guides and Directs from Above

Several minutes ago I saw a television ad suggesting people become foster parents. It catapulted me back to my first job out of graduate school at the Department of Children and Youth Services. I see myself back then, seated at my desk on a snowy day in 1984. It is pushed up against another desk. Vivian is looking at me. She has a fat face with slits for eyes. Dandruff sprinkles her shoulders. Looking around my desk I see fifty-eight case records. I feel disgust.

"No way," I mutter to myself. It's not possible that fifty-eight families will be helped. "No time." The repulsion is in my stomach and my brain. Suddenly, the phone rings. It is my mother. Her voice is like a breath of fresh air.

"Joanie, what are you doing tomorrow?"

"I am working."

"Could you take the day off?" she asks. "I need to get an eyeball in Pennsylvania."

"What?" I giggle. A day away from fifty-eight cases is a no-brainer, but the word *eyeball* is not computing.

"I won't be seeing out of that eye anymore," Mom explains. "I don't want to look ugly."

My heart sinks. Mom is in her early seventies, and she is a diabetic. A cataract operation has not been successful. The retina has detached, leaving her blind in one eye.

"Sure, Mutz (my nickname for her). I love you."

The next day I push the buzzer to her apartment in Massapequa, New York. I hear her feet across the floor above me, followed by a steady minute of buzzing. I laugh. She always wants to make sure I get in. She is smiling at her door and gives me a hug. Anne is dubbed "the crusher" for her hearty hugs. I am thankful.

Six hours later we are in Pennsylvania. We look at the gray stone building that manufactures eye prostheses. I see the "1800" cornerstone. The building is not dreary. A gray-haired man in his late fifties greets us. He is gentle, not morbid. I glance at Mom; she is happy, half excited, and very relieved about the prostheses. Mr. Ray shows us around his factory. Mom and I laugh when we see the conveyer belt. Eyeballs of all colors are starring at us. Mr. Ray looks at Anne's good eye. He shows us samples. She looks at me for agreement as she chooses one.

"Anne, if I may call you that, with this little wooden stick, you can put the new eye over the pupil of your blind eye."

I look, seeing if mom flinches at the word *blind*. She does not.

"Right here, Anne, there is a suction pad at the end of the wooden stick," he continues. "You remove the prostheses before bed."

On her second try, the prosthesis is in place. She smiles at me and gives me her crusher hug. I whisper, "I love you, Mom."

If we were home, we would be doing our "dance of joy"— hugging and dancing, hugging and dancing, embraced in a circle. Mom looks in the mirror; she is wearing glasses. She does not look blind.

Mr. Ray breaks the mood. "Anne, have you thought about using a cane?"

The look on her face says, *What? Are you out of your mind?* But she says, "No, I will not need a cane." Anne is tenacious. She always has been. She is indomitable without being domineering.

Looking out our kitchen window, the sun is shining, the sky is a beautiful blue, and Mom has had the prostheses for ten years. No one thinks she is blind. She is thrilled. The sky made me think of her. While her face crosses my mind, I say to Bill and Bill J, "Let's go surprise grandma." They look away from the two hundred toy trucks. Bill J continues talking. He holds up his hand, letting me know he has not finished his inventory. "And this Hess truck Papa gave me. And this one Aunt Marie and Uncle Bob gave me, and this one—"

My husband smiles at me. His eyes say, *Isn't he amazing?* Bill says, "If we leave in an hour, she'll be back from the mall, and we can all go to dinner."

"Yeah, Grandma will give me a present," Bill J adds.

We all laugh. Forty-five minutes later, we are driving from North Branford, Connecticut, to Massapequa, New York. We are in Massapequa by four o'clock. We are walking up the sidewalk where several seniors are sunning themselves. "How cute," they say. "How old is he?"

"Five," the three of us answer.

Bill's hand is on the front door. He pushes the buzzer and says: "I can't wait for the long buzzer." But there is no long buzzer.

"Try again," I say.

Bill pushes the button. No answer.

"She must still be at the mall," I conclude.

"Hey, why don't we go to the mall? Maybe we'll see her. And Bill J loves riding up and down the escalators," Bill says.

"Okay." I agree.

An hour later, we return to Clocks Boulevard. I push the buzzer—no answer. "Maybe she went to hear Johnny play," I suggest. My brother Johnny is a musician. He sometimes takes Mom to hear him play, especially to fancy places where her beam lights up the room. We decide to go to Cleary's, which is an Irish family pub. The music is lively. Fat ladies, skinny men, young people, stout men, and children are dancing and singing on the dance floor. We whip off our coats and join the group. The music and the yelps are loud. I motion to Bill to let him know I am calling Mom. No answer. I feel worried—like worms are crawling inside of me. At nine o'clock we say good-bye to our new Irish friends.

We go to Grandma's. She is not home. "Something is wrong," I say. "She would be home by now if she were with Johnny."

"Well, let's use the keys and go up," Bill says. I am holding my breath as we climb two flights of stairs.

"Mommy, is Grandma home?" Bill J asks.

"I hope so, cutie."

Bill knocks. There is no answer. He opens the door and goes inside. Tears are streaming down his face when he comes out. "She has passed."

I cannot believe it. It is why I have been staying in the hallway. I do not want to see her dead. I do not want to experience her lack of vibrancy. Anne is high energy. Although she is eighty-two, she is not old in my mind.

"I can't go in—not yet. I just can't," I tell him.

Sobbing, Bill's eyes direct me to our five-year-old son. I crouch down and say, "Sweetheart, Grandma is in heaven. Let's go outside for a while."

We do not want Bill J to see the medical examiner and the funeral director. Bill and I motion to each other that I will see Mom after they have left.

The air feels good on my face.

"Bill J, Grandma is in heaven just like Mufasa in *The Lion King*."[15] I cannot stop the tears.

"It's all right, Mom. You can lean your head on my shoulder and cry," Bill J offers.

"I love you, sweetheart."

"It's going to be okay," he assures me. "And when you die, Mom, I am going to cry too."

Purposeful Destiny

While hugging him, I think about what a beautiful soul he is. Bill and I trade places. I go up to see Mom. She looks like she is taking a short nap. The television is on. Her amber chair is pushed close to the television.

A month later, Bill J and I are getting bikes out of the shed. He looks straight up into the sky, and smiling, he says, "Hi, Grandma!" My mother is smiling big time.

———˜˜˜∽∞∽˜˜˜———

Three months later, I miss her physically, especially the "crusher" hugs, her scent, and the sparkle in her eyes when she told a story—like how she was introduced to God:

You know, Joanie, I was only four years old. I was standing in the living room. The rays of sun were coming up through the window, and I said, "What's that, Mama?" And my mother said—I can still hear her words in broken English—"Anna, that is God."

Her face was a glow. Anne was a catholic. She did not expend energy on the rules of the religion. God was light. God shown down on you. God was in you, and His light shone out of you. "Joanie, you are beautiful inside and outside," she would say.

I miss her so badly and ask her to visit me in a dream. I chuckle at the role reversal—me, waiting for a visit from her. "I know you're busy, Mom, but when you get a chance, can you please drop by in a dream?" Of course, nothing happens immediately. But several weeks after my request, I have the following dream/visit:

Mom is hugging me. I am kissing her. We are doing our dance of joy. Her hugs feel so good. Her face is radiant. She hugs Bill and Bill J. Anne loves the water. Bill rents a boat. All of us are talking at once. We get in the boat. We are rowing on a beautiful lake. No one else is on the lake. The sun is shining. The air is cool and feels refreshing as it hits our faces. Big evergreen trees surround the lake. Bill says, "Look, there is a house in the lake."

"Where?" we shout simultaneously.

"To the right," he says. "It is brick."

"Brick?" We look at each other questioning: "How can that be?" Our eyes move to the right. There is a small brick house sitting on a submerged island.

I wake up smiling. "Thanks, Mom, for your visit. It was great."

The morning proceeds as usual. Bill J, now a big first grader, and I are standing at the bus stop with Tyler, our dog. We see the big yellow bus. It is crowded. Bill J gets on. I pat Tyler, and we head off for our morning hike. We hike the Turkey Trail—a mountainous trek. We are approaching the entrance. The huge evergreen trees cool us. I see the large mounds of dirt and wild flowers that mark the trail's opening. I am undoing Tyler's leash when I feel a strong pull in my stomach. It is nudging me to walk somewhere else. I look around. Signs are posted: "No Hiking Beyond This Point." Tyler and I walk to the signs. We peer into dense woods. The pull is still there. I know I must disobey the signs.

Walking, Tyler is chasing wild turkeys. There are hills. The hills are paved. I feel excited, not knowing where the prohibited route will take me. We walk several miles. Finally, the road ends. I look in front of me. I see the exact lake from my dream, surrounded by large evergreen trees. I look to the right, and there is the small brick house submerged on an island in the lake. Tears fill my eyes.

"Thanks, Mutz. You're a doll. Thank you, God. You're incredible."

I have never seen this lake before. Never.

Purposeful Destiny

Janice comes to mind. I see her face and remember a previous group session. Her eyes tell me she is somewhere else—not in my office. I wait for her to come back. She looks around the room at the other members of the bereavement group and then glances at the wedding ring on a silver chain.

"Yeah, I've been reading different books," she begins. "They keep saying Mike (her deceased husband of thirty years) will visit me like in a dream. I keep thinking of that movie *Ghost*[16]—you know, where we *see* Patrick Swayze but Demi Moore doesn't. Well, I want to *see* Mike."

Looking at the lake now, I cannot wait to tell her.

I am arranging the chairs in a circle for the group and anticipating sharing the "lake" dream/visit and its aftermath with Janice. I see Monica, Todd, and others taking their usual places. I try not to look disappointed as I welcome others who are not Janice. Glancing at the clock, it is twenty to eight. She is ten minutes late.

"Okay, let's hit it!" I announce.

Chuckles bounce off us. Each person is sharing his or her feelings. We are thirty minutes into the group, and I have lost hope of seeing Janice when, out of the corner of my eye, I see her moving to her chair, mumbling, "I'm sorry."

A smile spreads through my body. An opportunity has not arisen to tell the story. I have stored it for another time, when Todd, looking at Janice, says: "I got *Ghost* off of Netflix. I wasn't sure if I'd like it. You know, I'd get jazzed up that maybe Gary (Todd's deceased brother) was standing next to me and when the movie was over I'd say 'Jerk, it's a movie!'"

He looks down and swings his head around to face me. "Joan, do you believe it's true?"

I assure him I do and tell the dream/visit and its replication. No one speaks. I do not break the silence; Janice does.

"How did you know she'd visit?" she asks, her voice filled with a mixture of anger and annoyance.

"I didn't know 100 percent," I explain. "I thought she might be busy doing other things, but she always tried her best to help me, just like Mike tried his best to help you. And because of the suit and black eye."

I tell the story of the suit and black eye to the group—a very short version of what I will remember during the leisurely ride home after the group session has ended.

Sitting behind the wheel, I am back in high school. It is my sophomore year. My feet are bringing me to my greenish locker. Kathy, who is very popular and a cheerleader, is telling Melanie, also a cheerleader, that she is wearing a linen suit.

"See, it's lined with silk—silk," she says as she opens the jacket.

"Holy cow."

Bam—the next day I take my saved allowances and buy yards of linen and silk. I walk in the back door. "Mom, I want a linen suit lined with silk. Kathy's got one."

Mutz smiles a big smile. She chuckles a little. She is surprised. "Gee, I've never made a suit before." Her eyes are bright. "Yeah, let's give it a go."

Mom jumps into the project. She sews the arms of the jacket backward. No problem, she rips them out and starts again. Two weeks later, I have a white linen suit, silk lined. I am the queen of Weldon E. Howitt High School.

I love Mom's unwavering support. Anne is tenacious and fiercely loyal to her children and husband. In sixth grade my favorite skirt was gray felt with a pink poodle. I am in line to get on the school bus. Roger, who likes me, pushes me into a puddle, and the skirt gets wet. The pink Poodle is now brown. Johnny, my older brother, punches Roger in the face. "Don't ever push my sister again."

When we get home, Mom sees my face. Her eyes travel down to my skirt. Johnny says: "This kid Roger pushed her down. I punched him in the face."

The doorbell rings after dinner. I look at my brother, and he looks at me. Mom opens the front door. Roger is standing on our stoop. His face is swollen with a black eye. His mother has a big coat on. Her face is scrunched up. She opens her mouth and says, "Look at this."

Mom, with an edge in her voice, says: "He should not push little girls in the mud."

She does not invite them in. The door is closed. End of story.

I feel the dream, and seeing the lake in "reality" was a miracle. Carol Smith says in *An Angel by Your Side*: "Sometimes not a miracle but just believing takes the greatest faith of all."[17]

Claire, a tiny woman with a warm smile, is a member of the bereavement group; she pulls me aside after the meeting and asks: "How did you get to believe relationships continue after someone you love dies? My brother passed last year, and I would give anything to have a hug from him."

"I grew up with the belief," I explain. "But it was also through a series of happenings, like the lake story I mentioned."

During our next group meeting, a new member introduces herself. "My name is Elena. My sister passed away three weeks ago."

The group ensues. Much time is spent listening to Elena. Each member tells her who they are grieving. I look at the clock. It is nine-thirty. "We have to wrap up," I say.

Elena gets up, walks over to Claire, and gives her a hug. "This is a hug from Sammy," she says. Elena did not know Claire's desperate wish was a hug from him. Claire turns her head, looks at me, and smiles.

It is the Sunday before my first birthday since my mother has passed into spirit. I have been thinking about Claire. I will ask Mom for a hug. I need to feel her presence. Bill, Bill J, and I decide to take a nap. I awake from the nap feeling irritable. I look around the living room floor where the three of us have slept. Bill fell asleep on the rug. Bill J had been sleeping on the couch pillows. I fell asleep on gray-and-white pillows off a second couch.

While sleepily making coffee, Bill says, "Joan, what are you going to do with these sunflowers? They have been here rotting in the bag." His voice is more rigid than usual.

I look at the sunflowers I picked from our garden. "I'll show you what I am going to do." I pick up the bag, open the dining room door, and fling them outside.

"Nice, nice." Bill is shaking his head from side to side.

I begin to sob. "I miss my mother. This is going to be the first birthday when I will not see her."

Bill, still annoyed, says to Bill J: "Give your mother a hug."

His little arms feel great.

———

My birthday is today. "Mom, please be with me today. Let me know you are celebrating it with us." The request sent, I walk down the stairs. I see birthday cards and a bag of new sunflower seeds on the table—a "smile" from Bill. Among my presents is a manila envelope with rolls of film that have been developed. Bill and Bill J have giggle eyes. They tell me to get dressed but will not tell me where we are going. We drive along; I see the sign for the Griswold Inn in Essex. The Inn is white. Outside is a horseless carriage decorated with pots of flowers. I walk in and notice the low ceilings and a fireplace. A waitress takes us to a table. As we pass, I notice part of the second room is metal. Could it have come from an old ship? A fire is aglow in the room where we are seated. There are prints of old ships and book-lined walls.

Bill hands me the manila folder. "There is no specific order. I just randomly selected films that have been there forever."

I laugh, and so does Bill. My hand reaches inside the envelope. I feel a piece of paper. I take it out. On the top in big block letters I see typed "GRANDMA MUTZ." My eyes scan the left where I read "WORLD'S BEST GRANDMOTHER" and her address. To the right, I recognize my mother's telephone number.

Enclosed in a white mat is a penny with my mother's birth year. I kiss Bill. "You're remarkable. Thank you." I reach into the envelope and take out the first package. I am excited. The pictures could have been taken before Bill J started school. I open the flap and take out the first picture. Mom is smiling with her prosthesis and big eyeglasses. I feel a sob in my throat; warm tears are on my cheeks. She heard my prayer and is with me on my birthday.

Bill J's voice is squeaky. "Why is Mommy crying?"

Bill reaches for his hand. "She is both happy and sad because she is thinking of Grandma."

The rough material of the napkin is absorbing my tears when the piano player plays "It Had to Be You." Turning to Bill, I ask, "Did you request that? It's my parent's courting song."

His eyes are mellow, and he leans closer to me. "No, I didn't know they had one."

Mom became "Mutz" when I was twelve years old. She and I were being silly. We were looking at a figurine, a mustached man playing an organ grinder.

"His name is Giorgio, and he has three cats," I surmise.

"No, his name is Gasper. He hates cats. He loves his donkey—Alfredo," my mom counters.

"Wait, wait—I got it. He loves his fat wife, Giovanna, and he bought Alfredo for her to ride on, so she could come out with him."

"Well, actually not only does he love his wife, Giovanna. But he loves his eight children, and he bought three donkeys so that everybody can go with him. But one donkey's belly is almost to the ground because he should have bought one more donkey!"

"Mom, you're a Mutzburger!" I blurt out.

We are laughing. We are slapping the table as the story gets bigger.

Anne is happy while on earth. I imagine she is more so in her spirit life. She is organized. Every morning as a child I awake to her tapping out a song on the oatmeal pot. Mom loves us and her husband.

It is three o'clock in the afternoon. I walk into the house through the back door. Because of the time, I know Mom is upstairs. I walk up sixteen stairs into my parents' room. Looking ahead, I see Anne seated at her vanity table with the big mirror. I smell her scent; it is like roses. She is combing her hair up. She is making little rows on the top of her head. Her hand reaches into the side drawer. Mom pulls out a coral flower and puts it in her hair. I see her look in the mirror. She smiles. She wants her husband to see her pretty.

"Oh, Joanie," she says as she sees me.

"Mom, you look beautiful."

Anne looks down and smiles shyly. "Daddy will be home soon."

Purposeful Destiny

Mom was content with her earth life. But it was not a Walt Disney sitcom. A favorite anonymous quote is: "It's not the weight of the burden but how you carry it."

It is 1988. Anne is looking at the first billing statement for my private practice. Her eyes are beaming. "Oh, Joanie, I'm so proud of you. I love to listen to your message on your machine. You sound so good—not like me with my Brooklyn accent."

"What Brooklyn accent?" I ask her. "You don't have a Brooklyn accent."

"Yeah, but I didn't go to college like you."

"So, so what—a banana could go to college, Ma. You don't have to be smart. You're one of the smartest people I know."

"Oh, Joanie." she hugs me.

I feel sad she disbelieves her intelligence; she is highly intuitive and very creative. Mom now makes patterns for dresses and suits. I am frustrated she doubts her smarts because she quit high school and did not go to college. Her biggest heartache is my brother's mental illness, which surfaced at twenty-one when he was diagnosed manic depressive that occasionally slides into schizophrenia. And no—no other noses got punched during his childhood and teenage years. As a matter of fact, in his later years, when on the proper medication, he worked and married. But Anne always worried she did something wrong.

"But, Joanie, what did I do wrong?" she would ask me.

"You didn't do anything wrong, and neither did Johnny. It's biological," I assured her.

"Biological?"

"Ma, if you urinated for a full minute, would you say, 'Wow, I'm a really great person'?"

She giggles.

"Or if you urinated for just two seconds, would you say, 'I'm not a good person'?"

"No—no, not at all."

"Well, it's just how some peoples' bodies are wired."

She cried mostly, because after many attempts, I knew it was dangerous for me and Johnny to be in the same room. One time he hallucinated I had made angry faces and gestures at him.

I am in Mom's apartment when the buzzer rings. Johnny is let in.

"You were making faces at me," he says. "You were raising your fists at me while we were driving home from the hospital."

"John, I didn't—honestly. I did not." My heart is pounding.

He lunges at me. Luckily, I get out of reach. Several months later, after a failed suicide attempt, he is banging Mom's head on the kitchen floor. Marie and I call an ambulance, and he is hospitalized.

Once he is out of the hospitable, Mom asks: "Can't you just forgive Johnny? Can't we just be a family all together?"

"I can't, Mom. You know I have tried many, many times to start over. But it's not a matter of forgiveness. It's a matter of accepting his disease."

She's got tears in her eyes.

"I'm sorry, Mom. This tears me apart. You know I would do anything for you. But I can't do this."

Anne does not have an attitude toward me. She does not lash out at me. Mom carries her burdens well. Thankfully, three years before Mutz passes away, Johnny is on a medication that has the best effect. We are reunited.

Mom does not say: "I told you so."

Years earlier, I am sitting in Mom's tiny kitchen, in a chair next to the only window. It is a senior citizen apartment. She has used her assets for Johnny's private hospitalizations. I worry about the roaches I occasionally see scurrying across her countertop, anxious she might not see them and inadvertently eat them.

Her response is: "So what? They're protein." She is saying: "*Sputa la fenestrate.*" (Spit out the window.)

It is 1980, and my heart feels sore. The ache brings me back to my time in Amsterdam.

Paul is one of the many new friends I made while in Amsterdam during a sabbatical I took from Herbert H. Lehman College to travel throughout Europe and North Africa. He is a journalist who also decided to broaden his scope through traveling.

I am sitting in the Engel Bavarda cafe. It is unlike an American bar or restaurant; the atmosphere resembles a household living room. Chessboards and newspapers are plenty. There is no push to buy more drinks or coffee. Paul is sitting across from me. He has blond hair and big, blue eyes.

His face is animated. "I heard the tourist information bureau is not sending info to the embassy because of the strike." (At the time, there is an international oil strike going on.)

"Oh?"

"The embassy says they'll endorse a tourist magazine." He looks to the side, and I notice a mischievous smile.

"And, of course, you're not interested, because you love writing on spec and having your articles stolen."

"Absolutely," he agrees.

"You're telling me because—?" I question.

"I thought you might be interested."

We agree to let me have a week to think about it.

The week has passed; we're at the same cafe. "Well, let's go for it. You write, and I'll be the idea woman," I suggest.

Paul is practically shouting. "Are you serious?"

"Yeah, but it should be a full-fledged edition. No mock-up, and it should be bilingual. The big guys will probably show up with mocks and slides; it's a small country." I was thinking of J. Walter Thompson.

"Yeah, but where does the money come from?" Paul asks me.

"Let's both scrape up what we can."

Our families cash in insurance policies. I land a job in the psychology department of the University of Amsterdam. Sitting in the tiny kitchen, my mind shifts to the presentation day. I see two twenty-eight-year-olds, straggly with a full first edition at the embassy. I look around; the big guys look glossy. No one notices us. We are last. My heart is pounding, and I am thinking: "Was this a crazy thing to do?"

Paul announces, "Joan, Joan, we got it!" We try to act mature, but outside we laugh and repeat: "This is unbelievable. This is unbelievable."

Later that night, Paul visits. He looks somber. "I don't think I can do this—I would be too happy." I find out he's not kidding. We stay longer but do not have the capitol to wait out the financing from the big corporations. The project is not completed, for the embassy endorsement is without financial backing. I return home, take a student loan, and enroll in graduate school for an MSW.

My mind comes back to reality—back to my mother's kitchen. Mom says again, "*Sputa la fenestrate*." She is serious. I rise; I feel my hands on the base of the window. My muscles stretch as I push it up, the salvia gathers, and I spit out the window. She smiles at me. I smile back and realize Anne has showed me how to carry a burden well.

It is 1999; seventeen years have passed since I have been awarded my master's in social work. Johnny and I are talking on the phone.

Purposeful Destiny

"I can't believe it's three years that Mom's been gone," he says. "I miss her."

"Yeah, I miss her crusher hugs, but I feel her presence around me. I mean, not all the time. Do you?"

"I don't know about 'presence'—that sounds weird to me, but I think about her."

The conversation ends, and I begin wrapping crystal glasses Mom gave Bill and I a year before she departed. The crystal glasses are part of what I am bringing to a surprise tenth wedding anniversary party at Nadia's. Nadia's is the Chuck E. Cheese equivalent for adults. I ask each of our friends to wear their wedding-day attire. Many respond by saying something similar to: "You're kidding. I'd need bungee cords to keep the clothes on."

"Then just dress as a wedding guest."

While wrapping the crystal glasses, I say: "Mom, please be with us. I so much want you to be there."

I am looking in the closet for something to carry the glasses. My eyes spot a nylon bag Mutz had used. My hand searches the bag to make sure it is empty. I feel a bulge. I look inside the bulge and see the little figurine—the organ grinder, the Mutzburger one. My heart leaps. "Oh, Mom, thank you. You're here."

The bag has been in the closet for three years. I never felt the figurine before.

Bill walks in and says, "I want to give you one of your presents now."

"Great."

He hands me a small package. Written on the wrapping paper are the words "I love you." I feel like Mexican jumping beans are inside of me. Tearing the paper off, I see a frame with porcelain angels. There is a picture of Bill and me on our wedding day with his one arm around me and the other arm around my mother.

"So there you are again," I say as I kiss the picture.

These "visits" from Mom make me think of a recent conversation with Claire. My hand is on the door ready to open it to start the bereavement group when I hear "Joan—Joan, wait up." I turn my head and see Claire sprinting toward me.

"I have to tell you something," she says. "A few days ago I told Sammy I'd love to hear Springsteen's 'Born in the USA.'[18] You know, we used to sing it on the top of our heads while driving in his car, and I wanted to sing it with him again. Late that night, I couldn't sleep, so I went for a ride. Guess what comes on the radio?"

We both say at the same time: "Born in the USA." We are laughing with joy.

I tell her about the organ grinder and Bill's picture.

"My God, this is too much," she says. "You know, some of my family thinks I've gone crazy."

"It might make them feel better if they read Dr. Raymond Moody's *Life After Life*," I suggest.

"Are there other ones you can think of?"

"Yes. *Talking to Heaven* by James Van Praagh and Dr. Louis LaGrand's *After Death Communication*."

"Even if they don't read them, I'll feel better—you know, armed with proof," Claire says.

"You mean you'll know you and I are not the only two people in the world who carry on conversations with our 'dead' relatives."

She chuckles and gives me a hug.

———

I am sitting in my office. It is supper time. I have four more clients to see. I turn around, and on the long wooden table behind my chair I see a picture of my mother and me. She is holding my hand as she is smiling at the camera while our hands are touching my grandparents' names engraved in a granite wall on Ellis Island.

Purposeful Destiny

"I love you Mutz," I say as I put her picture next to me while I am eating dinner. Looking at her face, I feel comforted. I take my last mouthful and say to her: "I have to get back to work."

I walk upstairs to wash my dinner dishes, passing the lawyers' offices above mine. I hear the fax machines. I am mindful of their privacy, but my eye catches the front page of a newspaper. The heading is: "Mommy's Little Girl." My breath stops.

"Mom, you are amazing. How did you do that?"

The Red Cardinal: A Caring Father Shows His Love through Unusual Visits

Matt, my father-in-law, is listening. His head is leaning forward as I continue telling my story.

"So, I'm coming out of the Regional Water Authority after Tyler and I have just finished the Turkey Trail."

Matt's nodding his head.

"Suddenly, I spot a Regional Authority cop's SUV. The cop steps in front of us and says, "You know, it's a $350 fine for not having a dog on a leash. I could fine you $350."

"Okay. You sure it's $350?"

"Look that's what I said." He's a young, skinny guy with a hat that looks just a tad too big for him. There is a pause. I let the pause go longer than usual.

"Or, you know, I could put you in jail for a day."

"Well, would jail be on a Monday?"

"What?"

"Would jail be on a Monday? Because I work on Mondays. Or, wait a minute, I could go on a Tuesday. But I could not go on a Wednesday, because, again, I work on Wednesdays."

Matt's face is smiling—a big smile. He dislikes small town policemen, especially since they fined him seventy dollars on a Fourth of July when he was setting off some fireworks for his grandchildren and family.

The cop's face is scrunched up and his eyes are wide. "Look, lady, just go and don't bring your dog on Regional Water property."

Matt and I are laughing. I am slapping my thigh and laughing hard.

Three years later, in 1999, I am retelling the cop story, because I know Matt likes it. I'm not sure it's heard, because he is heavily drugged. He is in hospice. He is dying of brain cancer. I am there at an off hour; thus, I am the only visitor. I see the small square sponge attached to a stick. I pour a fresh glass of water and put the sponge up to Matt's lips. His body color looks gray.

"I love you, Papa," I say to him. (He became Papa after his grandchildren were born.) I leave his side and walk out the front door of hospice feeling he will pass away soon. The first thing I see is a bright red cardinal in a mostly leafless tree. Looking at the cardinal, I say to myself, "Oh, Papa, I hope that's how you'll let us know your spirit is around us."

Papa passed away in the middle of that night, October 18, 1999. His five sons were the pallbearers. Alex, his eleven-year-old granddaughter, with her father, also named Matt, gave the eulogy.

One of Papa's requests before he went to hospice was that he would be remembered by his grandchildren. We are all gathered at Papa's house after the funeral when one of his stepsons comes into the sunroom and announces: "Look, the kids want to build a clubhouse for Papa. They are selling memberships to the clubhouse. No membership—no entry. So start coughing up the money."

We all laugh. Everyone reaches in their pockets. A week later, we are building the clubhouse. It's blue. It's tucked in a grove of evergreens.

———

Several weeks later, I am sharing the loss with the bereavement group. After the group, a small, dark-haired woman named Nancy, whose husband passed away at a track meet he was coaching, asks, "Joan, you're going to think I'm crazy—"

"No, Nancy, I won't. As you know, I'm 10 percent crazy."

"Well ..." Tears are rolling down her face, and she is looking down as she speaks. "Do you know of anyone who ... who can reach people on the other side? I feel crazy asking this—really."

"I don't know of anyone." I take her hand and look straight into her eyes. "But if I do hear of someone, I promise you that I will check them out. If I think they are authentic, I will give you their name."

"Oh thank you."

We hug.

A month later, Marlene, an attractive redheaded woman in her thirties who is not in the bereavement group but is a client, is sitting on the edge of the brown corduroy couch. She is jabbing the air with her index finger.

"Joan, Joan, you have to go see this woman Marti. She's the real thing. She connects people with their departed ones. I know you do a bereavement group. You've got to go."

"Marlene, I have never seen you this excited. I think it's the first time you ever sat on the edge of the couch!"

"Well, she's really good."

"Okay, but what's her last name?"

"It's some Italian last name—Del something or other. But I have her telephone number, and she just goes by Marti."

I remember my promise to Nancy. An appointment is made. I am driving on a cold November afternoon. I am feeling nervous. Will I find the house? Will I be able to keep a flat, expressionless face so that I do not give anything away?

"Just look for the red Mustang," Marti had told me. I see it. I am relieved. I walk up to the door. A woman with shoulder-length hair opens the door.

"I'm Marti's sister-in-law. Marti is still with someone. You're Joan?"

"Yes."

A few minutes go by, and she says, "You can go downstairs now."

I walk down a flight of stairs to a finished basement. *Oh God, this is eerie*, I think. Marti is seated at a card table. She has a warm smile and is very relaxed. She has brown hair; she is a big-boned woman and is wearing comfortable clothes. Folding chairs are set up in semicircular rows, ready, it seems, for an audience. I am trying to keep my face blank as Marti motions me to a chair. Her eyes are big and inviting, but I am determined to be nonresponsive.

Marti tells me I am a "healer." I don't respond. It is hard to keep my eyes dull. "Does St. Patrick's Day mean anything to you?" I feel my head move back. St. Patrick's Day is Papa's birthday. A series of images travel across my mind. One is of his "fat foot." He had been bitten by a dog, and his lymph nodes had been damaged. He was supposed to drain the water buildup with a special apparatus but never did.

I hear Marti repeat: "Does this mean anything to you?" Her face is calm, her smile is natural, and annoyance has not visited.

"Yes, it does."

"Well, your father-in-law is here."

"Oh, really?" *Ah. Oh, she's nuts,* I muse.

"Yes, he's trying to sit next to you, but he's having a difficult time getting into the folding chair because of his fat foot."

My face unglues.

"He's saying: 'Joan, remember the night I passed, and you came to visit me at hospice that day? You saw the red cardinal in the tree, and you said: "Oh, Papa, if that was only how we knew that your spirit was around us."

"Yes, yes." My pulse picks up.

"Well, I want you to tell all my sons I love them," Marti says. "And tell everyone that when they see a red cardinal, I'm there. Say hi to Davey, and I know Kate will be okay. There is no more pain."

Tears are rolling down my cheeks. "Oh, Papa, I'm so happy for you."

"And there are beautiful bells chiming—playing."

"I love you, and I will tell everyone."

Marti and I look at each other, and this time, our eyes lock. "You know, I intended to remain a blank tableau, but I melted."

She laughs. "I know. He was determined to talk to you."

"Thank you, Marti."

I walk up the stairs feeling excited and amazed; there is no doubt I have had a conversation with Matt/Papa.

Ambling to my car, it dawns on me that my then sister-in-law Kate was scheduled for an operation. Immediately, an alarm blares in my mind. *How am I going to tell all his sons? They'll think I'm crazy.* I feel a giggle in my throat and think, *They already think you're crazy!*

Starting the car, I recall trying to share a Wonder Bread truck story with Matt. His body language telegraphed "uncomfortable," but he graciously did not tell me I was insane.

Driving home, Matt's life travels across my mind. He was born in East Boston in 1932. His father (Matt Sr.) began as a janitor for the National Bank of Boston. He worked his way up to director of operations. His mother was a stay-at-home mom. The Hoeys, which included a daughter Amy (named after her mother), lived in a railroad flat. Extended family lived in the same house in separate apartments.

One evening, Matt's mom is passing the room of her six-year-old son, whom she nicknamed Sonny. She peeks in and notices his eyes are open.

"Sonny, why are you still awake?"

"Whenever I close my eyes, I think of Jesus, and then I have to bow my head."

"Well, it's time to go to sleep."

Mrs. McQueeny and Mrs. Millard, neighbors, are sure Sonny is going to be a priest. It's Sunday. Mrs. McQueeny and Mrs. Millard are watching Sonny at the altar. He is an altar boy. He is wearing a white blouse and a black top over it—a cassock. He is holding the big missal. He walks from the right side of the altar, genuflects, and brings it to the left side of the altar. Two years earlier, it had been too heavy for him to carry. Father McCarity is saying mass. Mrs. McQueeny's and Mrs. Millard's eyes follow him. They are sitting in the third pew on the left-hand side of St. Mary's Star of the Sea Church. They turn look at each other, their eyes telegraphing: *Father Hoey. Start sewing.*

Each week Matt's parents make a twenty-dollar deposit in Noodle Island Cooperative Bank for Matt's college education. They are holding hands as they stop at Kelly's ice cream, part of the weekly ritual. Satisfaction is flowing through them as they eat their ice cream, believing their son will go to college.

Nine years later, Sonny is holding an envelope. The return address reads "Boston College." He tears it open. He sees the word he wants: *accepted*. Matt and Amy are thrilled. During orientation, Matt Jr. overhears a guy saying: "Yeah, he's a day-hopper. You know, he's not living in the dorm." The submessage is "he's poor, he can't afford the dorms." Matt pretends not to hear the comment and says to himself: "Yeah, but I'll graduate."

While in college, he gets a job at the Boston Public Library. Matt rushes there from ROTC practice. As he is putting his jacket on the coat hook, he sees a girl with creamy skin, brown hair, and a gorgeous smile. He learns her name is Mary Jo. *I will definitely know her*, he thinks to himself. During the next few months, they talk and flirt. Mary Jo tells her best friend, Beth, that Matt is very good looking. He has sandy-colored hair, big blue eyes, and a great build.

When he asks her to go ice skating, her answer is yes.

Matt says, "Saturday?"

"Yes, Saturday would be fine." Mary Jo immediately tells Beth.

Saturday afternoon arrives. The sun is shining. The pond is frozen. Matt is helping Mary Jo put her skates on.

"I'm pulling the laces tight for better support. Tell me if I'm hurting you."

She smiles down, taking in his blondish hair and big blue eyes. "No, no, not at all. They feel fine."

The cold air feels good on their faces as they skate. Their overcoats are keeping them warm. They have a good repartee going on. It's an exceptional day. Matt glances down and sees a crack in the ice. In a nanosecond, they both fall in the lake. They look at each other horrified and then laugh.

"We've got to get you home," Matt says, and he hails a cab.

The cab stops at a house on Common Wealth Avenue, the wealthy section of Boston. Mary Jo's father opens the door. He sees that his daughter's overcoat is soaking wet, as well as everything else she is wearing. Standing next to her is a young fellow. He is soaking wet. Mr. Quigley's face is frown-covered.

Matt says, "Hello, I am Matt Hoey. I took your daughter skating. The pond cracked unexpectedly. I am so sorry."

Seeing how sincere Matt is, Mr. Quigley says,

"Just bad luck. Let's get you some dry clothes."

Mary Jo is relieved her father is taking this well.

Matt, knowing he has no money to pay the waiting cab, asks: "Mr. Quigley, can I pay you back for the cab outside?"

Mr. Quigley smiles. Matt does pay him back.

Through his life, Matt is known for his genuineness. A sentence he often says is: Do the next right thing.

During a group visit at hospice, in 1999, visitors marvel when, through a medication haze, Matt utters, "I should be doing something."

"Get an A in resting," I respond.

Matt valued his intellectual curiosity and ability. However, like all of us, he had fears. One of them was confrontation. I recall a time when I began to relay the lyrics of "In the Living Years"[19] by Mike and the Mechanics, which depicts a son's frustration at the inability of father and son to communicate emotions. Matt walked away. Another time he joked about the irony of being a counselor (he was also an engineer and an educator) who had difficulty expressing deeper emotions.

Matt and Mary Jo marry. They are the first in the extended family to move out of Massachusetts, and they settle in Old Saybrook, Connecticut. They have five sons. It is a busy life. A cousin in Massachusetts tells Bill at a family gathering in 2010: "We thought you guys were rich. I mean, we said, 'My God, they've got a freezer—a freezer in their house with lots and lots of popsicles.'"

Everyone laughs.

But Mary Jo and Matt are "rich." They are on the same page. Each is an ardent Catholic. All the boys go to Catholic elementary school. Three out of five sons go to Catholic high school. It is hustle and bustle—hustle and bustle.

One day, their seven-year-old son, Billy, comes home from his paper route and announces: "Mom, the McFarland's aren't married."

"What makes you say that?" Mary Jo asks.

"Well, because they eat by candlelight."

Mary Jo chuckles to herself and later tells her husband they're married because they don't eat by candlelight. Matt looks in her smiling eyes.

"And who gave you that information?" he asks.

"Billy."

Bang-bam—the next night, the Hoeys are eating by candlelight. Mary Jo is a doer with a sense of humor. Matt adores her. They are buddies, and they parent well.

Mary Jo teaches at the elementary school where Billy is in second grade. Mrs. Carol, the principal, calls her down to the office. Seven-year-old Billy is there.

"Tell your mother what you did."

"I stuck a lead pencil in Mark's butt."

Mary Jo's eyes penetrate Billy's. She then looks at the principal and utters, "Thank you," while ushering Billy out. Once the door is closed, she asks: "Why?"

"Well, it was reading time. Mark takes forever to read, Mom—*forever*. He can't pronounce the words. He ruins it every day. So I took my pencil and stuck him in the butt. You know, to move him along. Is he going to die from lead poisoning?"

"Who said that?"

"The principal."

"No, he won't die. But you can't do this again."

Later that night, most of the boys are gathered in the kitchen. Matt is about to take them out to play baseball. He catches Mary Jo's signal to talk. Outside, Matt hears his wife say: "Billy stuck Mark's behind with a pencil." Giggles are stifled. A "baldy" at Naldo's is the agreed punishment.

Billy is seated in a big chair at Naldo's Barber Shop. Naldo knows it is a punishment when Matt orders a baldy, for he has just given the other boys regular haircuts. Naldo is a short, dark-haired Italian man with a mustache. His little barber shop is a fixture on Main Street. Billy does not look in the mirror as Naldo shaves off his hair. He tries to not listen to what Naldo is saying.

"You know, Billy, see that trap door?" He is pointing to a section of the floor. "I keep a bear down there. He's very quiet, because I just fed him a squirrel and a bucket of honey."

"I don't believe you," Billy says.

"It's true, Billy. Sometimes I worry the latch on the trap door won't hold him."

Billy wants out. He is wondering: *Is there really a bear down there? No ... that's stupid ... Maybe.* The baldy completed, Naldo hands him a comb. *I hate Naldo. He's nuts,* Billy thinks. He feels relief moving through his body when they get on Main Street, which is already showing signs of Christmas. Stores have lights and Santa displays.

Matt is a lector at church. His sons often hear his voice from the pulpit. Mary Jo has been working with the Ladies' Guild to prepare the church for Christmas. She loves Christmas and has also decorated the house to the hilt—two Christmas trees, one for the boys' ornaments and one for her and Matt.

Eight weeks later, Mary Jo is diagnosed with cancer. Matt and Mary Jo are crying in each other's arms. She insists she will beat it. Matt honors her wishes to not tell the boys the cancer diagnosis. They all had been told, as Mary Jo had been told, that she had asthma. Weeks later, she passes away.

Matt keeps her clothes in the closet for twelve years. He feels like an amputee. He cannot talk about her. Two years later, he is making dinner for his sons, who also have been shell-shocked by their mother's death. That night's meatloaf

Purposeful Destiny

with bacon on top is finished, and Matt takes it out of the oven. The boys have set the table. They all sit down. They are about to say grace when Matt gets up quickly and reaches into the freezer; remembering boys are supposed to eat vegetables, he breaks open a frozen box of squash and puts it on the table. It is the right thing to do. He also manages to go to some of his son Matt's football games and to stand at a designated spot at Billy's track meets so when Billy passes in his long-distance event he will see Dad.

A month after my visit with Marti, I took two weeks off to work on this book. The night before the first day, I wrote a letter to God.

Dear God,

Thank you for enlightening my mind when I work on the book tomorrow. Thank you for your divine light coming straight through me if you know it's for my highest best. Thank you.

I love you,
Joan

I put the letter in my God Box, a decorated shoe box with a slot cut in the cover, and envision it is mailed to my Higher Power. The next day the writing goes so well that I decide to write a second letter to God when a picture of Papa with his second wife, who he married in 1984, and their extended family falls off our library shelf. Smiling, I pick up the picture and say: "I got the message." I crumple the paper.

The following morning, I am sitting in our dining room. Four feet away from the windows, a red cardinal sits in a tree. I feel encouraged; I am on the right path. I feel joy. My mind shifts to members of my bereavement group.

I hear myself saying to them: "Imagine the happiness you and your departed loved ones would feel saying hi to each other. Your departed love ones want you to be happy. The relationship is, of course, different when we cannot see them, when their physical bodies are not in front of us. But over time, as their presence is acknowledged, you will be amazed how often they are with you and help you. Their spirit and love for you is here. There is a bridge across forever; it is widening your mind and hearts to connect with theirs on God's highway—love"

The two weeks of writing ends. My life is busy. I have compressed a five-day practice into three days: Monday, Tuesday, and Saturday. On Wednesday, Thursday, and Friday, I pick Bill J up from school and bring kids home with him. Because he is our only child, I make a commitment to have other children in the house. Our neighbors' children are grown up.

Today, Nicky and Tommy are over. They are playing Superman in the living room, taking chances jumping off the living room couch. I comment on the leaps. After they have exhausted themselves, we all eat ice cream. I take them home.

Afterward, Bill J and I go grocery shopping. Between unpacking the groceries and beginning dinner, I answer client calls and contact insurance companies. Dad comes home. After dinner, the three of us play soccer outside. It's Bill J against Bill and me—the geezers. Of course, Bill J wins. His nine-year-old face is beaming.

"It's getting harder to let him win," Bill whispers.

We go inside, ready to begin the homework drill. Looking at Bill, I say: "I'm pooped." I realize as I am uttering the sentence that I need more alone time with my husband.

The next day, Bill says, "I was going through Papa's stuff (a box of papers and folders) and look what I found." He hands me a picture of Papa as a much younger man shaking his opponent's hand after he was elected assistant selectman of Old Saybrook. My eye notices a poem stapled to the picture.

I smile at Bill. "The Rose," I say aloud.

Bill's face telegraphs what he is thinking: *Isn't that something?* "Our wedding song."

"Yeah, I didn't know it was a favorite of his."

"Wow, just last night I was feeling I needed more alone time with you."

"Well, Papa agrees, and so do I. How about DC this April?"

Two weeks later, we are in a hotel with two adjoining rooms—one for Bill J and one just for us.

While recently talking with my brother-in-law Dan, reminiscing when I relayed Papa's message to him and his brothers and their families, I said: "I bet you thought I was whacked."

Dan laughs; he is a good-natured man and honest. He looks at me, the light in his kitchen highlighting his red hair. "Yeah, I did think you were whacked. But then when I was making a difficult move years back, I looked out in the yard, and there was a red cardinal. It stayed there for the *entire move.*"

Often we hesitate to tell others about visits with our departed loved ones for fear we will be considered off-kilter. Certainly, I was nervous sharing Papa's request with his sons. But only our Higher Power knows when it will be relevant to others. Actually, more books are being written depicting the belief that it is not the departed person who severs the relationship, but the bereaved, for they do not believe these bridges exist or fear they will be thought odd if shared. Dr. Louis LeGrand, Dr. Raymond Moody, James Van Praagh, Dr. Michael Newton,[20] and others have written about such communication.

Papa's visits are not only apparent through the presence of a red cardinal. On the eve of traditional holidays, I wish all my departed loved ones Happy Christmas, etc., because that is the time I acutely miss them physically. In 2002, I wished them a Happy Easter. Waking up the next morning, Bill excitedly tells me he has found a picture of Papa and I holding hands the Easter before he passed away. Again, he did not know that the night before I wished his father a Happy Easter.

While drinking my morning coffee and smiling about the hello from Papa, members from different bereavement groups cross my mind. Emma takes center stage. I see her sitting at almost the top of the circle the group has formed. She is in her midsixties and attractive. The gold wedding ring she wears on a chain is highlighted by her black sweater. All eyes are focused on her, because for the first time, tears are flowing.

She says: "You know, each holiday season I would make my special cake covered in chocolate frosting. Each year Fred (her husband of thirty-five years who is now deceased) would try to sneak a taste of frosting, and I would slap his hand. Well, last night I was making my usual holiday cake. My daughter and grandchildren were not home. As a matter of fact, no one was home. I finished putting the frosting on the cake. I turned around after putting the knife in the sink, and I saw a large fingerprint in the frosting. It felt like my heart stopped. Remember, no one else was in the house. I checked my ring to see if it had brushed the frosting. There was no frosting on it. Fred was there. I know he was there. He wanted to let me know he was there."

Our loved ones in spirit know what will hit home. They know how we feel. Dr. Michael Newton depicts the deceased trying to comfort their grieving families. I decide to schedule a second appointment with Marti to validate that our loved ones in spirit hear us and are very much "alive." I elect to ask Papa to share something only my husband, Bill J, immediate family members, and I would know. Marti greets me warmly. She had moved to a beautiful house, and the sun is shining through large windows as the session begins.

Marti laughs softly. "I don't know why he's saying tattoo," she says.

"Because I want him to tell me something only Bill, Bill J, immediate family, and I would know. Bill has a tattoo on his hip."

Before asking a prepared question, my mind shifts to the day I was scheduled to talk to a bereaved staff at an inpatient Alzheimer's facility where nine patients passed away in a short period of time. Driving without a GPS device, I made a wrong turn. Panicking, I glanced at the dashboard and simultaneously saw that the gas was low and it was 11:52 a.m. Knowing my presentation was scheduled for noon, I yelled: "Papa, help me. I've got to get there on time." Amazingly, I arrived with ten minutes to spare.

And so I ask aloud, "Papa, the day I asked for your help to get me to the Alzheimer's facility, did you hear my prayers?"

"I did hear you. I do hear you. I heard your prayers that day. You were also concerned about running out of gas, as you were trying to find your way. I knew what was up. There was the gas thing going on and your stress about getting there. But you made it there safe and sound and with time to spare. I don't feel you were late or anything."

"Oh, Papa. No, I was not late. I was amazed when I looked at the clock, and I was ten minutes early. Thank you."

Papa knew his son Bill was wondering if he was angry with him for wearing an embossed pin that read "I Survived Catholic School" during teenage years. The thought crossed Bill's mind before an initial interview with a Catholic-funded agency. In the same way, he knew his sister Amy needed support during the Christmas of 2010 when her dear friend was diagnosed with cancer and when I worried if Bill J would be accepted into Wentworth Institute of Technology, his preferred choice. He visited each of us in his usual way. His hellos supported us and, in each instance, foreshadowed a successful destiny.

A frequent sentiment during bereavement groups is: "I must be strong for my kids/grandkids." For people this often translates: "I won't talk about [the deceased person], because I don't want to upset those around me. And certainly I don't want them to see me cry."

This is my response: "Sad isn't bad."[21] Talking about departed loved ones, tearful or not, gives others permission to express their feelings.

On August 14, 2012, Bill J graduates from Wentworth. We arrive the day before the ceremony. Aunt Amy asks to see his graduation cap and gown after he shows her around his apartment. He opens the closet, shows the gown, puts the cap on his head, and then turns it over. Inside is a picture of Papa.

Epilogue

Bill and I will be celebrating our twenty-fifth wedding anniversary on February 18. He is still my special friend whom I love.

Bill J is a graduate student in architecture at Wentworth Institute of Technology in Boston. His portfolio has received good reviews.

Carl is happily married, and he tells me consulting himself is automatic, as is stating his opinion and saying no when warranted. He laughingly told me he gets much practice with his teenage daughter. Carl informed me he regularly converses with God directly and does not feel he has to ask saints or other intermediaries to intercede for him.

Gabby married the man she met through the dating service. They are expecting their second child. She wrote recently that she no longer asks God a thousand times for something, because after the third time, she notices the bump on her head.

My father still reassures and steers me. Anne recently visited me in a dream and imparted: "Write the book *now*." Her forcefulness surprised me, for although dynamic, she is not domineering.

Amy, Matt's sister, while on the grounds of a second senior housing complex, trying to choose, saw a red cardinal and thanked her brother for a decision made.

Obstacles, unusual circumstances, a strong pull in the pit of the stomach, synchronistic happenings, and the guidance of our departed ones are all God's ways of directing us, for His love is deep and forever.

Endnotes

1. John Prine, "A Good Time," *Sweet Revenge*, January 24, 1990, Atlantic.
2. Shirley Christian, "For Peru's New Chief, a Litany of Ills," *New York Times*, July 28, 1990, http://www.nytimes.com/1990/07/28/world/for-peru-s-new-chief-a-litany-of-ills.html.
3. Ibid.
4. Sandhills Sixteen, "I've Been Working on the Railroad," 1927, Victor Records.
5. Shirley Christian, "Baby Trail Is Leading Couples to Peru," *New York Times*, August 16, 1990, http://www.nytimes.com/1990/08/16/garden/baby-trail-is-leading-couples-to-peru.html.
6. Betty J. Eadie, *Embraced by the Light* (New York: Bantam, 1994), 103–104.
7. Raffi Cavoukian, "Must Be Santa," *Singable Songs for the Very Young*, 1976, Shoreline.
8. Bill McKibben *Maybe One* (New York: Simon & Schuster, 1998).
9. Sylvia Browne, *Conversations with the Other Side* (California: Hay House, 2002), 101.
10. John B. Turner, Robert Morris, Martha N. Ozawa, Beatrice Phillips, Paul Schreiber, Bernice K. Simon, Beatrice N. Saunders, *Encyclopedia of Social Work Volume 1* (Washington, DC: NASW, 1977), 632–633.
11. Ray Bradbury, LifeQuoteslib.com
12. Raffi Cavoukian, "Down by the Bay," *Singable Songs for the Very Young*, 1976, Shoreline.
13. Michael Newton, *Destiny of Souls: New Case Studies of Life between Lives* (St. Paul: Llewellyn Worldwide, Ltd., 2000), 150–152.
14. Sylvia Browne, *Life on the Other Side: A Psychic's Tour of the Afterlife* (New York: Penguin Putnam Inc., 2000), 80–84.

15 *The Lion King*, directed by Rob Minkoff and Roger Allers (1994; Walt Disney Pictures).
16 *Ghost*, directed by Jerry Zucker (1990; Paramount Pictures).
17 Carol Smith and Wallis Metts Jr.,(Publications International Limited, Ltd. 2002) An Angel by Your Side: Thoughts for Each Day.
18 Bruce Springsteen, "Born in the U.S.A.," *Born in the U.S.A.*, October 25, 1990, Sony.
19 Mike and the Mechanics, "In the Living Years," *Living Years*, October 28, 1988, Atlantic.
20 Michael Newton, *Destiny of Souls: New Case Studies of Life between Lives*. 11–49.
21 Michaelene Mundy, *Sad Isn't Bad: A Good-Grief Guidebook for Kids Dealing with Loss* (Somerset, Crewherne, Southwest, UK: Abbey Press, 1998).

Readers Guide

1) Do you believe you have been guided to destinies purposeful for you? If so, what were they?
2) Reviewing your life examine "Unusual happenings" you have experienced.
3) Consider the times you believed your prayers were unheard. Was belief lost? Did it return? What were the circumstances?
4) Share opinions and experiences about "departed" loved ones desires to maintain their earthly relationships.
5) Is it possible to heal a difficult relationship, with the participation of a departed loved one, after "death"?
6) When choosing a life partner how essential is physical attraction? What other qualities are important? When would you consider them?
7) Are there consequences for not stating your opinion in a committed relationship? Is it more compassionate to be honest?
8) Share when a leap of faith was taken. What were the results? How did you feel before and after?

About the Author

Joan Hoey, LCSW, earned a Masters in Social Work from Adelphi University, and has more than twenty years of clinical experience as a private practitioner, trainer, and human service consultant. She has lectured at Herbert H. Lehman College of the City of New York and the University of Amsterdam, Holland having been a full time faculty member at both Universities.

She and her husband, Bill reside in Northford, Connecticut. Their son Bill J resides and works in Boston, Massachuesetts.

Made in the USA
Middletown, DE
04 March 2017